the italian grill

Clarkson Potter/Publishers
NEW YORK

Micol Negrin

the italian grill

fresh ideas to fire up your outdoor cooking

Published by Clarkson Potter/Publishers, New York, New York

Member of the Crown Publishing Group, a division of Random House, Inc.

www.clarksonpotter.com

CLARKSON N. POTTER is a trademark and POTTER and colophon are
registered trademarks of Random House, Inc.

Printed in Singapore

Design by Jane Treuhaft

Food and prop styling by Roscoe Betsill

Library of Congress Cataloging-in-Publication Data

Negrin, Micol. The Italian grill: fresh ideas to fire up your outdoor cooking / Micol Negrin.

Includes index.

1. Cookery, Italian. 2. Barbecue cookery. I. Title.

TX723.N4596 2005

641.5'784'0945—dc22   2004020103

ISBN 1-4000-5422-2

10   9   8   7   6   5   4   3   2   1

First Edition

to my parents,
Mony and Gabriella,
for making me
who I am

and to
my husband, Dino,
for making
every day
a celebration

contents

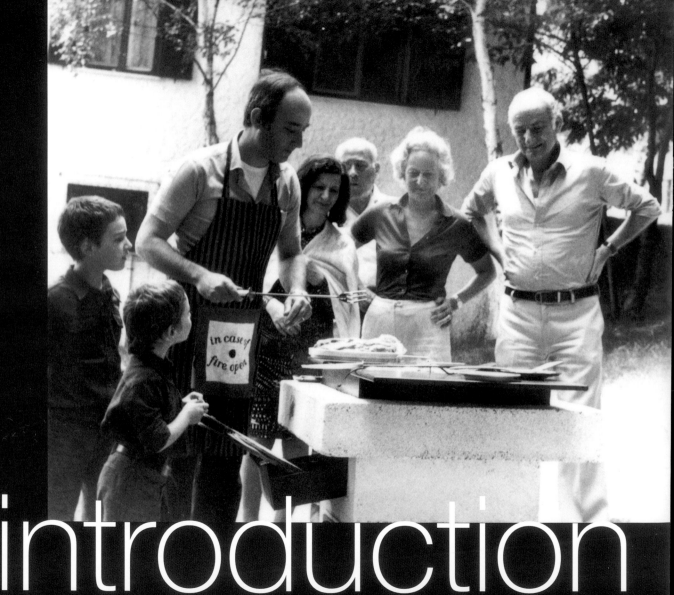

introduction

there's a black-and-white photo of my family in the seventies:

my father in his striped apron with a fork in hand, my grandmother in a shimmery summer shirt, my grandfather peeking playfully over her shoulder, various great-uncles and great-aunts long since gone, me with a pixie haircut, my brother in the background, all of us standing by a squat cement grill under a cherry tree. My mother is nowhere in this photo—she is probably in the kitchen, getting a platter of skewered meats or cut-up vegetables—but her presence is palpable, and we are all awaiting her return, looking at the grill in hungry expectation.

This photo, which still hangs in my parents' hallway more than thirty years later, captured many things: an ordinary moment in the life of a family, always more precious in retrospect; a moment in history, when bell-bottoms and smoking at the table were the norm; and, to me at least, the feeling of being a child again, of anticipating the first bite of something I've watched sizzle on the grill for what seems like far too long.

At our weekend home overlooking the Lago Maggiore, my parents had an outdoor grill built so we could cook simple foods for friends and family. The menu was almost always the same, but none of us minded. We had beef sausages laced with garlic, skewers threaded with bright red cubes of peppers and chunks of glistening meat, and finger-thick slices of bread we rubbed with a peeled clove of garlic as soon as they came off the grill. We had big, juicy steaks, strips of zucchini, coins of eggplant. The kids drank water, the adults wine, and a meal that on nor-mal days would end by two in the afternoon dragged on peacefully into the early evening hours. When the grill was lit, ordinary rules no longer applied. We ate outside, let the day slide languorously by, and cleared the table only when we felt like it.

Whenever I ignite a grill, I remember those days and the sense of tranquillity they engendered. Maybe that's why I've always loved to grill. Or maybe it's just something inside all of us, a reaching back to the days when humans first domesticated fire, cooked a piece of meat over the glowing flames, and discovered how delicious bits of charred flesh could be.

Whatever the reason—personal or primeval, or a happy mix of both—grilling strikes me as the perfect way to cook almost anything. It's just you, food, and fire. There's a simplicity to the equation that is pleas-ing. And as long as the ingredients are perfect, the results are bound to be spectacular.

Throughout the Mediterranean, grilling has long

been a popular cooking technique. In Italy, almost every cook has his or her favorite grilling recipes, traded like family secrets around the dinner table and passed down from generation to generation like prized jewels. Some cooks brush sausages with a rosemary branch dipped in vinegar as they sizzle over the fire. I vividly recall when I first saw this, at an unpretentious family-run trattoria in a tiny hilltop town in Calabria, and I can still taste those sausages and marvel at how moist they emerged from their fire-bath. Others insist that the marinade for chicken *alla diavola* must include oregano, and others still throw myrtle branches into the smoldering embers to imbue lamb or rabbit with an earthy aroma.

From region to region and town to town, Italian cooks have learned to harness the power and the allure of the grill to create fabulous fire-kissed feasts. And although some of these recipes are prepared in restaurants across Italy—like bruschetta (country bread brushed with olive oil), spiedini misti (mixed skewers), and tagliata alla griglia (sliced steak)—a good number of grilled specialties remain the domain of home cooks.

Why? Because grilling is easy, quick, and relatively mess-free. Whether you have an honest-to-goodness charcoal grill, a gas grill, or an electric grill, the effort is minimal—and the possibilities are endless. When I gathered recipes for this book, I sought out preparations both traditional and innovative for every course, from antipasto to dessert, that highlight the Italian penchant for simplicity, seasonality, and great flavor. Some are world-famous specialties, like Florence's grilled T-bone steak showered with slivered arugula, and some are humble staples, like grilled polenta; some are new to the American scene, like fire-grilled focaccia stuffed with mascarpone and truffled olive oil, and some are novel spins on old favorites, like prosciutto-wrapped grilled figs. All will bring a fresh, vibrant taste of Italy to your table.

grills

The recipes in this book were tested on a variety of grills: charcoal, wood-burning, gas, electric, and even grill pans. As long as you regulate the heat and keep in mind a few key techniques (see Tips for Successful Grilling, page 12), any grill will produce fabulous food.

charcoal and wood-burning grills

These grills provide the strongest heat and the most intense smoke flavor, and it is easier to toss aromatic wood chips or herbs over live coals or wood than into the smoker box (if there even is one) of a gas grill. On the other hand, they also require more work to get the flame going and to control it throughout the cooking process. Although many home cooks use self-lighting charcoal, you can also opt for an electric starter (an electrical coil that is set under a pile of charcoal) or a chimney starter (a tall cylinder in which coals are lit, then dumped beneath the grill grate). If using a wood-burning grill, use only hardwood (oak, apple, hickory, mesquite, cherry), as soft wood (fir and pine) produce far too much soot.

gas grills

Gas grills are much more predictable than charcoal or wood-burning grills: You turn on a switch and there's your flame. Before turning on the grill, be sure to open the lid (unless the manufacturer's instructions indicate otherwise); starting a gas grill with a closed lid may produce gas buildup and cause an explosion. Because most gas grills have a tough time getting really hot, it's a good idea to preheat them for at least five to ten minutes before starting to cook.

electric grills

Like gas grills, these are far more predictable than charcoal or wood-burning grills. However, they rarely attain very high temperatures and are best suited to cooking small or thin cuts of food that cook through rather quickly.

grill pans

The final option for apartment dwellers is a handy grill pan. These are small enough to fit in a drawer, easy to clean, and inexpensive. The best have high, clearly defined ridges that not only produce visible grill marks, but allow grease to drip down, away from the food. I like steel or cast-iron grill pans best. Always run the vent on top of the stove to clear out smoke when using a grill pan.

additional grilling equipment

If you grill on anything other than a grill pan, you will need the following:

Stiff wire brush, for scrubbing the grill grate
Heavy grill gloves
Grate grabber, which resembles pinched tongs, and is used to lift the hot grate from the grill
Drip pans, for placing under food to catch the drippings when grilling indirectly (see page 13)
Grill baskets, which come in an assortment of shapes and sizes and are ideal for fish, diced vegetables, even cheese sandwiches

And to turn or test food on the grill (including a grill pan), you will need:

Long-handled tongs
Long-handled basting brushes
Meat thermometer
Skewers: wood or metal, but wood must be soaked in water to cover for thirty minutes to prevent burning
Spatulas

tips for successful grilling

control the heat

on a charcoal or wood-burning grill The most challenging aspect of grilling, particularly over live flames, is controlling the heat. In general, thin cuts of food (steaks, strips of zucchini, fish fillets) require high heat for a short period of time; thick foods (leg of lamb, whole fish, certain bread doughs) call for less intense heat over a longer period of time, or the outside of the food may burn before the inside has a chance to cook through. With this in mind, here are four ways to control the heat so your food turns out evenly cooked.

1. The heat is strongest immediately after all the coals have ignited (they will be orange). If you want to start the food over an intense heat, place the food on the grate at this point. To cook the food over a less intense heat, wait until the coals start to ash over (they will be white). The longer you wait, the cooler the fire will become.

2. Rake the coals into a thin layer for a lower heat, or into a thicker pile for a more intense heat. Or, better yet, build a three-zone fire: Spread the coals in a double layer in one area, in a single layer in another area, and finally, leave a third area coal-free. Move the food from the hottest zone (on top of the double layer of coals, ideal for searing and getting good color on the outside of large pieces of meat), to the medium zone (on top of the single layer of coals, ideal for prolonged cooking), to the cool zone (where there are no coals, but indirect heat will continue to warm and finish cooking food) as needed to control how quickly the food cooks.

3. Lower or raise the grill grate closer to or farther from the heat. Food cooks through faster when it is close to the heat; the best grills have a height-adjustable grate.

4. Open or close the vents. When the vents are closed, oxygen is cut off, and without oxygen, flames are stifled and coals become extinguished. When direct grilling, close the vents at the top when you want to lower the flame; open the bottom vents to prevent too much smoke.

on a gas or electric grill Controlling the heat on a gas grill is much easier than over charcoal or wood. Gas grills with powerful burners can be set up with a three-zone fire: Turn one burner on high, one on medium, and one on low, and move the food over the three zones to cook it more or less quickly as needed. Gas grills with lower outputs have a tough time getting hot enough, so don't bother with the three-zone fire on such grills; instead, preheat your grill for a full five to ten minutes before placing the food on it, so it has enough power to really sear the food. Remember: Small cuts of food do well over brisk heat, while thick cuts must be cooked low and slow or the outside will char before the inside has a chance to cook.

direct versus indirect grilling

There are two ways to grill food: directly and indirectly. When you cook food right over a live fire or a hot flame, you are grilling it directly; the heat is intense and aimed right at the food. But when you pile the coals on either side of the grill and cook the food on top of the unlit portion, you are grilling the food indirectly—a great way to cook large cuts of meat or even whole fish, which require more diffuse heat and low, slow cooking to emerge moist and char-free from the grill. To grill food indirectly, always cover the grill, and maintain a medium temperature.

wipe off excess marinade

If you marinated food in a liquid-based marinade, wipe off the excess marinade with paper towels before placing the food on the grill to avoid flare-ups and to achieve clearly defined grill marks.

keep the grill grate clean

Cooking on a dirty grill causes the food to stick and gives it a bitter, burned taste, so always keep your grill grate clean. Use a stiff, long-handled wire brush to scrub the grill grate both before and after grilling. Scrub once after you've preheated the grill but before you put any food on it, and a second time after grilling, while the grill is still hot. It's much easier to clean a grill when it's hot, as the heat sterilizes the grate and loosens any stuck-on bits.

oil the grill grate

Be sure to lightly oil the grate before placing food on it. This will not only prevent sticking, it will result in more prominent grill marks. There are three ways to oil the grill grate: spray with an oil can (do this while holding the grate away from the grill, or you may cause flare-ups); rub with a slab of bacon or pork fat (hold it steady between a set of long-handled tongs); or rub with a rag soaked in oil (again, hold the folded rag with a set of tongs).

to marinate or not to marinate

Whether or not to marinate meat, fish, or any other food before grilling has as much to do with time constraints as it does with the final result you want to achieve. Marinades are used to flavor and to tenderize food; they can be liquid or dry, oil-based or acid-based, and can contain any number of herbs, spices, and other seasonings (for more on marinades, see sidebar on page 16). Preparing a marinade is easy, and it can be done fairly quickly if you have all the ingredients on hand—but then the food has to marinate, something you might not have the time (or patience) for. Meat, especially red meats and game, benefit from prolonged marinating time; a day or two in a flavorful marinade only improves their texture and flavor. But fish and seafood, which are already tender, are better marinated only briefly; marinating too long turns them mushy.

When time is short, use dry rubs to lend additional flavor to food; the recipes on pages 156–157 are ideal for last-minute preparations. Or, if you want to marinate a cut of meat in a liquid marinade, toss the meat with the marinade and let it sit at room temperature up to two hours, instead of refrigerating it up to two days: Marinades penetrate food much more effectively, and quickly, at room temperature. If you marinate meat, fish, or seafood at room temperature rather than in the refrigerator, do so for a maximum of two hours, as bacteria multiply much faster at warmer temperatures.

spice rub ingredients for meat and poultry [RECIPE PAGE 157]

BLACK
PEPPERCORNS

WILD FENNEL

DRIED
RED PEPPER FLAKES

SEA SALT

DRIED OREGANO

Marinades not only flavor food, they also serve as tenderizers. There are two main types of marinades: liquid and dry. Liquid marinades generally contain oil, acid (lemon juice, vinegar, or wine), and aromatic ingredients (herbs, spices, garlic, and so on). The oil carries flavor from the marinade through the permeable walls of the meat and tenderizes it. Extra-virgin olive oil contains monoglycerides, natural emulsifiers that help the oil penetrate the meat deeper and faster, and is therefore a perfect choice for marinades. Acids such as wine and vinegar break down tough cuts of meat and game or fowl; some recipes call for soaking meats in acid-based marinades for days to achieve a more tender texture.

Dry marinades (also referred to as rubs) are based on herbs, spices, and salt.

Unlike meat and poultry, fish and seafood don't benefit from prolonged marinating: Their delicate flesh breaks down and starts to become mushy as a result of the acid in the marinade. Keep this in mind when marinating fish and seafood:

1. Prepare simple marinades (3 or 4 ingredients are usually enough) so you don't overwhelm the flavor of the fish.

2. Marinate fish and seafood no longer than 30 minutes to avoid breaking down the protein and making the texture unpleasantly soft.

3. Acid in a marinade causes the protein to become firmer and to take on an opaque appearance (as though it had been cooked). But that doesn't mean that fish and seafood that is anything but impeccably fresh and sushi-quality should be eaten raw after marinating.

4. Before grilling, blot marinated fish thoroughly dry to prevent it from sticking to the grill.

And remember: If you didn't have time to marinate your meat or fish before grilling it, you can still lend additional flavor after it's cooked by drizzling raw extra-virgin olive oil over it, or by sprinkling it with freshly squeezed lemon juice just before serving. Chopped fresh herbs, a bit of freshly ground black pepper, or a few drops of aged balsamic vinegar are also great last-minute flavor boosters.

before you cook

Great food starts with great ingredients. And the simpler a dish, the more all-important the quality of the ingredients. Since grilling is all about simplicity, you just can't get by with anything less than good raw materials: There are no heavy sauces to mask an inferior cut of meat, no drawn-out cooking times to hide an old or insipid vegetable. Buy only the best ingredients available, and try to cook seasonally (after all, is there a better time to eat tomatoes than in the summer, a better time to indulge your appetite for asparagus than in the spring?).

Before you fire up the grill, read the recipes you'll be preparing all the way through. This will prevent annoying last-minute surprises, like finding out you should marinate the chicken for two hours before cooking it, or that you need a potato ricer or cheesecloth for a given step in the recipe. As for substitutions, most are fine, and I urge you to trust your instincts. This is how we become creative in the kitchen and develop our own cooking style.

You'll notice that almost every recipe in the book calls for olive oil, all but a handful (some of the desserts) require salt, and most savory recipes (and a few sweet ones) include herbs. A few words of advice on these essential ingredients.

olive oil

Use only extra-virgin olive oil. It has the lowest acidity content of all olive oils (a maximum of 1 percent) and is never chemically extracted; only mechanical pressure is applied to squeeze the precious golden liquid out of the olives. If you don't use extra-virgin olive oil all that often, store it in the refrigerator to slow down oxidation; return it to room temperature before using it. If you use it often, store it away from heat and light; a cool pantry cupboard will do. For more on olive oil, see page 141.

salt

All recipes in this book were tested using kosher salt, which has a cleaner flavor and is less salty than iodized or table salt. Fine sea salt is also delicious: It has a lovely marine flavor, and falls somewhere between kosher and iodized or table salt in terms of saltiness. If you are using iodized or table salt rather than kosher salt, you need to scale down the amount of salt you add by one third. And remember: Always taste a finished dish before bringing it to the table, so you can adjust the seasoning if needed. No matter how arduously I test my recipes, my tomato might have been smaller than yours, my flame higher, your lemon more tart than mine . . . and the list goes on and on. All of these factors will affect the final flavor of a dish. So taste, taste, taste before serving.

herbs

I adore fresh herbs, and I use them abundantly every chance I get. All the recipes in this book, unless otherwise noted, call for fresh herbs. Dried herbs can sometimes be substituted (in lesser amounts than fresh, and only in the case of certain hardy herbs like thyme and rosemary), but there is nothing like the aroma of fresh-cut herbs permeating your kitchen and your food. Keep versatile herbs like Italian (flat-leaf) parsley, basil, sage, and thyme handy; if you must substitute the dried stuff for the fresh, cut the amount by half.

antipasti

grilled ham and cheese with marinated mushrooms *panini al formaggio, prosciutto cotto e funghi* 28

thinly sliced seared salmon with white truffle oil, three peppercorns, and chives *fettine di salmone con olio tartufato, tre pepi ed erba cipollina* 30

smoked swordfish "carpaccio" smothered in arugula *"carpaccio" di pesce spada affumicato con rucola* 32

tomato-rubbed bruschetta *bruschetta al pomodoro* 20

asparagus spears wrapped in pancetta *involtini di asparagi e pancetta* 21

bruschetta with chopped tomatoes, tuna, and capers *bruschetta con pomodoro, tonno e capperi* 22

skewered scamorza and bread in warm anchovy butter *spiedini di provatura* 24

figs enrobed in prosciutto *fichi avvolti nel prosciutto* 25

young goat cheese and smoked prosciutto coins *caprini alla griglia avvolti nello speck* 27

tomato-rubbed bruschetta

bruschetta al pomodoro /// SERVES 4

Twelve ½-inch-thick slices of
  country bread (½ pound total)
4 garlic cloves, peeled
4 ripe, juicy beefsteak tomatoes,
  halved along the width
¾ cup extra-virgin olive oil, plus
  extra if needed
Sea salt to taste
12 basil leaves (optional)

cook's note You'll be left with all that
gorgeous tomato flesh once you've
finished preparing a platter of this
bruschetta. Why not dice it and sauté
in olive oil with a bit of slivered garlic
and a few thyme sprigs until it becomes tender, and serve alongside
grilled fish or with pasta.

It's no coincidence that this quintessentially simple recipe is first in the book: Whenever I get an irrepressible craving for food cooked over a live fire, this is the one dish I can't do without. Country bread is thickly sliced; grilled until it is browned on the outside but still moist inside; rubbed with a peeled garlic clove first, then with a juicy tomato; and finally drizzled with fruity olive oil and seasoned with sea salt.

Heat a grill to a high flame.

Arrange the bread in a single layer on the grill and cook until the bottom is nicely browned but not burned; turn and cook until the other side is also nicely browned. It will take 1 to 2 minutes per side, depending on how hot your fire is.

Arrange the bread on a serving platter. Place the garlic, halved tomatoes, olive oil, salt, and basil (if using) on the table.

Show everyone at the table how to flavor their bruschetta: Take a slice of grilled bread, rub it lightly with garlic (just a few strokes— don't overdo it, or the garlic flavor will overpower that of the bread, olive oil, and tomato), then rub with the cut side of a tomato half until the seeds pop and the juices run out, moistening the bread amply. Drizzle with the olive oil, sprinkle with salt, and, if desired, top with torn basil leaves. Savor immediately, before the bread becomes soggy.

bruschetta in the olive mill **In its simplest expression, bruschetta is nothing more than bread grilled over an open fire, drizzled with olive oil and sprinkled with salt. In fact, a slice of bruschetta was used for the traditional testing (and tasting!) of the year's newly pressed olive oil. After days of laborious gathering and pressing of the olives, the farmhands and land-owners stood in the mill and dipped a slice of grilled bread into the green-gold liquid in ceremonial silence. Gar-lic was never rubbed on the bread, for it would interfere with the oil's fla-vor, and tomatoes were never added. This was a solemn moment, much like the moment a cask of wine was tapped: All the year's hopes and ef-forts were distilled into that first taste, that first bite of bread dipped in oil.**

asparagus spears wrapped in pancetta

involtini di asparagi e pancetta /// SERVES 4

20 medium asparagus spears

¼ teaspoon salt

¼ teaspoon freshly ground black pepper

2 tablespoons extra-virgin olive oil

20 thin slices of pancetta

cook's note If pancetta—an Italian unsmoked bacon, often rolled rather than flat—is unavailable, use bacon instead.

White or green, it doesn't really matter: Whichever asparagus you prefer will be fine in this easy antipasto. Just be sure to select asparagus with tightly closed tips and firm, unblemished stems—the signs of freshness. Avoid very thick asparagus, which wouldn't have the time to cook all the way through on the grill before the pancetta burns.

Heat a grill to a high flame.

If you are using wooden skewers, soak 8 skewers in water to cover for 30 minutes. Drain.

Meanwhile, place the asparagus spears on a cutting board with the tips lined up at the top. Cut the asparagus from the bottom so the spears are 4 inches long.

On a plate, combine the salt, pepper, and olive oil. Roll the asparagus in the olive oil mixture to coat evenly. Wrap 1 asparagus spear in 1 slice of pancetta, holding the seam side of the pancetta closed with one finger. Thread the wrapped asparagus on 2 skewers, puncturing the asparagus ½ inch from the tip with one skewer and ½ inch from the bottom with the second skewer. On the same two skewers, thread 4 more wrapped asparagus in the same way. You will have 2 skewers that are jointly holding 5 asparagus. Proceed in the same manner with the remaining asparagus and pancetta, making 4 double skewers containing 5 wrapped asparagus spears each. (The purpose of the skewers is to prevent the pancetta from unrolling.)

Grill the asparagus until the fat on the pancetta has melted and the pancetta is cooked, about 5 minutes, turning often to cook evenly; the asparagus should still be crunchy and the tips just tinged with brown. Serve hot.

bruschetta with chopped tomatoes, tuna, and capers

bruschetta con pomodoro, tonno e capperi /// SERVES 4

2 ripe, juicy beefsteak tomatoes
   (¾ pound total), cut into
   ¼-inch dice
½ small purple onion, cut into
   ⅛-inch dice
One 6-ounce can tuna packed in
   olive oil, drained and crumbled
¼ cup salted capers, rinsed,
   chopped if large
12 oil-cured black olives, pitted
   and cut into ⅛-inch dice
2 tablespoons minced oregano
½ teaspoon salt
¼ teaspoon freshly ground black
   pepper
2 tablespoons extra-virgin olive
   oil, plus extra if needed
Twelve ½-inch-thick slices
   country bread (½ pound total)
2 garlic cloves, peeled

cook's note The bruschetta topping is also wonderful as a cold pasta sauce. Simply boil 1 pound of pasta, drain it, reserving ½ cup of the pasta cooking water, and toss with the tuna mixture in a large bowl, diluting with some of the reserved pasta cooking water if needed.

I first tasted this embellished bruschetta in Sicily, where tuna and capers are both pantry staples. Serve it as a light summer lunch, or cut the bread into smaller pieces and pass around as finger food before a formal dinner.

Heat a grill to a high flame.

In a bowl, toss the tomatoes, onion, tuna, capers, olives, oregano, salt, pepper, and olive oil. Taste and adjust the seasoning if needed.

Arrange the bread in a single layer on the grill and cook until the bottom is nicely browned but not burned; turn and cook until the other side is also nicely browned. It will take 1 to 2 minutes per side, depending on how hot your fire is.

Rub the grilled bread lightly with the garlic. Arrange in a single layer on a serving platter. Top with the tomato and tuna mixture and serve within 15 minutes, before the bread becomes soggy.

tuna, an italian staple Tuna fishing is big business in Sicily and Calabria, and the waters of the Strait of Messina that divide the two regions are teeming with imposing bluefin tuna. In the warm spring and early summer, the bluefin swim to the Mediterranean to spawn. The Sicilians and Calabresi, skilled fishermen since the days of ancient Greece, catch them in an intricate set of interconnected underwater nets called tonnare following a ritual known as la mattanza: The last chamber of netting is the "death chamber," and it is here that the fishermen harpoon the tuna before hoisting them aboard the ships. While some of the tuna is sold fresh, especially to Japanese buyers, most of it is cooked in boiling water and salted, then packed in cans, where it can be kept for years. Think of oil-preserved tuna not as a compromise or as a substitute for the fresh stuff, but, rather, as a specialty in its own right. There's nothing like it atop green salads, paired with canned beans for a quick pasta sauce, or puréed with capers and butter as a delightfully easy spread for crostini.

skewered scamorza and bread in warm anchovy butter

spiedini di provatura /// SERVES 8

4 tablespoons (½ stick) unsalted
  butter
2 salted anchovies, boned,
  gutted, and rinsed, or
  4 anchovy fillets packed in oil,
  drained
2 tablespoons whole milk
1 loaf of country bread, cut into
  2-inch cubes
¾ pound scamorza cheese,
  cut into 2-inch cubes
2 tablespoons extra-virgin
  olive oil

cook's note Scamorza is a lovely pear-shaped cheese with a melting texture that belongs to the same family as mozzarella, caciocavallo, and provolone. If you can't find it in your local cheese shop or Italian market, opt for a young provolone or caciocavallo.

This seductive appetizer is a specialty of Rome and the countryside of Latium. Even if you aren't an anchovy fan, try the anchovy sauce that is poured over the skewered cheese and bread: It is the essence of the dish. It's important to use a relatively firm cheese like scamorza or young caciocavallo, and avoid soft cheeses like mozzarella, or the cheese will lose its shape and melt in puddles on the grill.

Heat a grill to a medium flame.

If you are using wooden skewers, soak 8 skewers in water to cover 30 minutes to prevent burning later; drain. Meanwhile, in a small saucepan over low heat, melt the butter with the anchovies until the anchovies dissolve. Stir in the milk and set aside.

Thread the cubes of bread and scamorza onto the skewers, alternating them and starting and ending each skewer with bread. You may not need all the bread and/or scamorza.

Grill until the scamorza melts somewhat but still holds its shape, about 10 minutes, brushing with the olive oil as it cooks.

Arrange the skewers on a platter and pour the warm anchovy sauce over them. Serve immediately.

not all anchovies are created equal If you've never tried a salted anchovy, you're missing out on one of the tastiest little nibbles around. Salt-packed anchovies are softer, suppler, and less spiny than their oil-packed counterparts. They are typically sold in tin cans and need to be rinsed of the excess salt before they are used. Once they are thoroughly rinsed, split them in half lengthwise to separate the two fillets, pull out the spine and any small bones (I use my fingernails for this task; a paring knife will also do), and rinse again. Blot dry thoroughly, and you're ready to enjoy your salted anchovies in any recipe that calls for them. One salted anchovy is equivalent to 2 anchovy fillets packed in oil. My favorite way to savor salted anchovies is atop bread that's generously slathered with unsalted butter.

figs enrobed in prosciutto

fichi avvolti nel prosciutto /// SERVES 4

12 fresh, ripe figs

12 paper-thin slices of prosciutto
di Parma, fat still attached

cook's note When fig season passes,
you can try dried figs instead of fresh.
Plump the dried figs in dry red or white
wine to cover for 15 minutes, then drain
and proceed as below. The recon-
stituted dried figs will take a few minutes longer than fresh ones to cook, so
move them to a cooler part of the grill if
needed to prevent the prosciutto from
burning.

The classic pairing of figs and prosciutto—a duet almost as common as melon
and prosciutto—lends itself well to the grill. The prosciutto enrobes the figs
even more snugly after cooking, and the sweetness of the figs is accentuated
by contact with heat. Enjoy with a refreshing glass of Gavi di Gavi.

Heat a grill to a high flame.

Meanwhile, wrap each fig in a slice of prosciutto, leaving the
stem end peeking out above the prosciutto.

Grill the figs until the fat on the prosciutto has melted and the figs
have started to soften, about 2 minutes; the prosciutto should be
lightly browned all over. Do not cook too long, or the figs will fall
apart on the grill (especially if they are very ripe). Serve hot.

the contrast game One of the cor-
nerstones of good cooking the world
over is the ability to create contrasting flavors. Good cooks naturally
strive for contrast, creating layered
taste combinations that stimulate
and titillate the palate. And so we
find creamy mozzarella coupled with
sweet, delicately acidic tomatoes;
bitter chocolate mousse topped with
tufts of sweetened whipped cream;
figs or melon paired with salty prosciutto . . . When creating a menu,
think of how the flavors within each
dish will contrast with one another—
and aim for contrasting textures as
well for the most satisfying eating
experience.

a memorable goat cheese **When I was little, my parents built a country house in Piedmont, about twenty minutes in the hills above Lago Maggiore. Every Friday night, after an hour-long drive from our home in Milan, where we lived during the week, we stopped at the local gastronomia in Arona, the city closest to our house in the hills. Two brothers, just as often short-tempered as they were kind, owned the shop, and you couldn't walk in there without buying *something*. There were fresh pastas filled with wild mushrooms or pumpkin; long, thin sausages and fat salami threaded with gleaming white fat; imposing hams; colorful fruit mustards and relishes; salads of seafood and rice; and, of course, an astoundingly aromatic array of cheeses both fresh and aged. My favorite were creamy, blue-veined gorgonzola, which I ate without benefit of bread as accompaniment, and little rounds of goat cheese called caprini that became wonderfully soft on the grill. The caprini of Piedmont can be as small as a thimble or as large as a hockey puck. Some are very creamy, barely aged a few days, while others acquire a slightly fuzzy, soft rind and are matured for months in special caves. All can be grilled; the important thing is to use moderate heat under the cheese so it won't burn on the outside before the inside has a chance to soften.**

young goat cheese and smoked prosciutto coins

caprini alla griglia avvolti nello speck /// SERVES 4

4 thin slices of speck, fat still attached

Four ¼-pound rounds of young goat cheese, about 2 inches in diameter (caprino in Italian)

4 cups packed mâche (lamb's lettuce) or mesclun (mixed baby greens), washed and dried

½ teaspoon salt

¼ teaspoon freshly ground black pepper

¼ cup extra-virgin olive oil

1 tablespoon red-wine or apple-cider vinegar (optional)

cook's note When buying speck for this recipe, be sure to ask whoever's slicing it to keep some of the fat on. If it's entirely defatted, it will dry out on the grill. Also, you don't want paper-thin slices here; again, you want to prevent the speck from dessicating on the grill.

Speck is a wonderful smoked prosciutto from the Austrian- and German-influenced northern region of Trentino–Alto Adige, which borders Austria. It has a particular affinity for mild, creamy, tangy cheeses, such as mascarpone, young robiola, and fresh goat cheese. In this recipe, I wrap coins of young goat cheese (domestic will be just fine if Italian is hard to find) in thin slices of speck, creating a sort of cheese-and-speck tournedos. (Remember tournedos? Those plump medallions of filet mignon wrapped in bacon?) The cheese is then grilled until the speck's fat starts to melt a bit and the cheese itself becomes soft and creamy, if not quite melted, on the inside. I serve the cheese atop young greens tossed with fruity olive oil—a perfect antipasto for a summer dinner.

Heat a grill to a medium flame.

Meanwhile, wrap the speck around the sides of the goat cheese rounds, leaving the top and bottom surfaces of the goat cheese rounds uncovered.

Arrange the goat cheese rounds on the grill and cook until the fat from the speck starts to melt and the cheese becomes a bit softer to the touch, about 3 minutes. Turn upside down (unless the cheese is too young to turn, in which case it will feel very fragile and is best left undisturbed on the grill as it finishes cooking) and cook 3 more minutes on the other side.

In a bowl, toss the mâche or mesclun with the salt, pepper, olive oil, and vinegar if using. Mound on 4 plates. Top each serving of salad with a goat cheese round and serve immediately, while the cheese is still hot.

grilled ham and cheese with marinated mushrooms

panini al formaggio, prosciutto cotto e funghi /// SERVES 4

Eight ¼-inch-thick slices of white
   bread
¼ cup extra-virgin olive oil
½ pound fontina cheese from
   Val d'Aosta, thinly sliced
¼ pound thinly sliced prosciutto
   cotto
1 cup oil-preserved mushrooms,
   drained and thinly sliced
1 tablespoon white truffle olive oil

cook's note Oil-preserved mushrooms are available in Italian markets
and specialty shops; if you can get
your hands on porcini rather than the
more common button mushrooms, try
them for a luxurious treat. If you can't
find oil-preserved mushrooms, opt for
oil-preserved artichokes, peppers, or
eggplants, or check the Mail-Order
Sources (page 183). Prosciutto cotto is
a cooked ham from Italy; baked ham is
a fine substitute.

Visit almost any café in Italy, and you will find an array of sweet and savory foods to nibble on between meals. These can range from something as simple as potato chips and marinated olives to more elaborate creations, like bite-size pastries and dainty panini. Known as tramezzini, these small panini are often triangular, built on white, untoasted bread, and sport a multitude of fillings: tuna and mayonnaise; prosciutto or salami; mozzarella and tomato; crab or shrimp salad. Those containing cheese are often grilled (these are usually my favorites). Office workers, window shoppers, and anyone out strolling will pop into the cafés (called bars in Italian), select the tramezzino of their choice for a quick energy fix, and eat it standing up at the counter, perhaps with a glass of wine or mineral water

This is the grilled ham and cheese of my childhood: I enjoyed it for a mid-day snack at the beach and nibbled on it at the corner bar while my parents drank their afternoon espresso. For a crisper texture, be sure to flatten the panini while they grill; I use a heavy spatula to do this.

Lay the slices of bread on a work surface. Brush one side of each slice with the olive oil. Flip 4 of the slices of bread so that the side you brushed with the olive oil is facing down, and top each of these with one quarter of the fontina, one quarter of the prosciutto cotto, and one quarter of the oil-preserved mushrooms.

Top with the 4 remaining slices of bread, placing them so that the side you brushed with the olive oil faces up.

Heat a grill to a medium-high flame.

Grill the panini until the bread is golden on the bottom, about 3 minutes. Turn and flatten with a heavy spatula; this will make for crisper panini. Cook until the other side is also browned and the fontina has melted, about 3 minutes. Remove the panini to a cutting board and cut each in half on the diagonal, creating 2 triangular wedges per panino. Drizzle with the white truffle olive oil. Serve hot, wrapping the bottom of each wedge in a paper napkin.

about truffle oil **Few ingredients evoke as much passion as does the precious truffle. Already prized by the ancient Egyptians, truffles have been considered not only food fit for kings, but an aphrodisiac, for thousands of years. The most precious truffle of all is the *Tuber magnatum pico,* an intensely aromatic white truffle native to Piedmont and the Marches in Italy. This fragrant fungus grows spontaneously in a symbiotic relationship with hazelnut and oak trees and cannot be cultivated—which partly explains its exorbitant cost, which hovers around $1,500 per pound (or as high as $3,000 in years when the weather doesn't cooperate). If you can head to Piedmont in autumn, make it a point to feast on fresh white truffles. Otherwise, you can revel in the aroma of white truffle oil, a fragrant oil infused with fresh white truffles, year-round. Look for the words *Tuber magnatum pico* on the bottle to be sure you are buying an oil infused with the precious white truffle and not a cheaper, less aromatic truffle; check the expiration date on the bottle, since oil oxidizes over time; and store the oil in the refrigerator to slow down deterioration. Return the oil to room temperature before using, and drizzle sparingly over grilled focaccia, fish carpaccio, risotto, soup, pasta, pizza, and more. But be careful: a little goes a long way.**

thinly sliced seared salmon with white truffle oil, three peppercorns, and chives

fettine di salmone con olio tartufato, tre pepi ed erba cipollina /// SERVES 4

½ teaspoon pink peppercorns

½ teaspoon green peppercorns

½ teaspoon black peppercorns

¾ teaspoon salt

½ pound sushi-quality boneless and skinless salmon fillet (from the thick part of the fillet, closer to the head if possible)

2 cups packed mesclun (mixed baby greens), washed and dried

2 tablespoons extra-virgin olive oil

2 tablespoons fresh lemon juice

2 tablespoons white truffle olive oil

¼ cup snipped chives

cook's note Pink peppercorns aren't peppercorns at all; they are the mildly pungent buds of a native Brazilian plant, *Schinus terebinthifolius* (true pepper belongs to the *Piper nigrum* plant). Green peppercorns are the unripe seeds of black pepper, available dried or in brine. White pepper is simply soaked black pepper stripped of its pericarp and pulp.

Salmon and truffles have a particular affinity for one another—and when chives and pink peppercorns are added to the mix, the flavor becomes deliciously layered and complex. Although the salmon is raw in the center, the outside is seared, which will make cutting it into very thin slices a challenge. But even if the slices look less than perfect, don't despair: The flavor will be incredible.

Heat a grill to a high flame.

Meanwhile, in a mortar with a pestle (or use a spice grinder if you prefer), crush the three kinds of peppercorns until they crack and just start to pulverize. Do not grind the peppercorns to a fine powder. Combine the pepper mixture and ½ teaspoon of the salt in a small bowl; rub all over the salmon, coating it well.

When you are ready to serve, in a large bowl, toss the mesclun with the remaining ¼ teaspoon of salt and the olive oil. Mound on a large platter.

Grill the salmon until it is just marked with brown on the outside, about 30 seconds per side, turning once. The salmon will still be raw in the center.

Cut the salmon on the diagonal into very thin slices; this may prove difficult, but do your best. Arrange the salmon slices around the mesclun on the platter. Drizzle the salmon (but not the mesclun) with the lemon juice first, then with the truffle oil, and scatter the chives over it. Serve immediately.

smoked swordfish "carpaccio" smothered in arugula

"carpaccio" di pesce spada affumicato con rucola /// SERVES 4

1 bunch of thick-stemmed
   rosemary sprigs

12 bay leaves

1 pound swordfish steak (about
   1 inch thick)

⅓ cup plus 1 tablespoon extra-
   virgin olive oil

¾ teaspoon salt

¼ teaspoon freshly ground black
   pepper

1 bunch of arugula, washed,
   dried, and stems removed
   (see Note)

3 tablespoons fresh lemon juice

cook's note Arugula's leaves are pleasantly pungent and peppery, but its stems are bitter. To prepare arugula for use in salads or as a garnish, wash well, dry thoroughly, and stack with all the stems facing in the same direction; cut the stems just where they meet the leaves, and discard.

I got the idea for this elegant appetizer from a pizzeria that my parents frequent in Piedmont. The chef slices smoked swordfish very thin, arranges it in a single layer on a chilled plate, and tops it with very fine strips of arugula. A lemon half, a cruet of olive oil, and a pepper grinder are served alongside so each diner can dress his or her salad to taste. I decided to replicate the subtle flavor of smoked swordfish on a grill. Just be sure to cook the swordfish over low, indirect heat, or it will dry out and burn before it takes on a smoky flavor. Calling this dish a carpaccio is taking creative license—after all, carpaccio was first made with raw beef, not smoked fish. But the presentation is reminiscent of beef carpaccio, hence the name.

If using a charcoal grill, pile the coals on either side of the grill, place a drip pan in the center underneath the grate, and scatter the rosemary sprigs and bay leaves over the coals. If using a gas grill with a dedicated smoker box, place the rosemary sprigs and bay leaves in the smoker box; if using a gas grill without a dedicated smoker box or an electric grill, place the rosemary sprigs and bay leaves on a sheet of aluminum foil, fold into a tightly sealed rectangle, poke a few holes in the foil pouch, and place the pouch directly over a burner under the grate.

Heat the grill to a medium flame. If using a gas grill, heat one burner to high and the others to low.

Rub the swordfish with 1 tablespoon of the olive oil, ½ teaspoon of the salt, and ⅛ teaspoon of the pepper.

If using a charcoal grill, place the swordfish on the grill over the drip pan and close the lid. If using a gas grill, place the swordfish over a low burner. Cover and cook for 15 minutes, or until the swordfish is lightly browned on the bottom and cooked all the way through. Remove the swordfish from the grill and cool to room temperature.

Slice the swordfish as thin as possible on the diagonal. Arrange the slices in a single layer on each of 4 chilled plates.

Make the arugula chiffonade: Stack 10 or so leaves of arugula at a time, roll into a tight bundle, and cut into very fine strips using a sharp knife. Repeat until you have cut all the arugula. (The same technique can be used for any green leaves: basil, spinach, chard, and so on.)

Scatter the arugula over the swordfish on the plates. Drizzle evenly with the lemon juice, then with the remaining $1/3$ cup of olive oil. Season with the remaining $1/4$ teaspoon of salt and $1/8$ teaspoon of pepper. Serve immediately.

the original carpaccio It was in Venice that Giuseppe Cipriani, owner of Harry's Bar, created the dish that has become such a classic of Italian cuisine for one of his regular clients, a Venetian countess. The countess's doctor had prescribed a diet based largely on raw meat and, hoping to make her monotonous meals more exciting, Cipriani sliced raw beef filet as thin as prosciutto and drizzled it with a mayonnaise and mustard sauce. He dubbed his creation carpaccio after the painter Carpaccio, whose canvases were echoed by the rich reds and yellows of Cipriani's dish and whose works were currently on exhibit in Venice. Today the name carpaccio is loosely used to describe any thinly sliced raw meat or fish (or even vegetable).

pizza,
focaccia,
and other primi

grilled polenta coins with creamy gorgonzola sauce *polenta alla griglia con salsa al gorgonzola* 46

smoky flatbread *torta sul testo* 48

neapolitan calzone *calzone alla napoletana* 50

focaccia stuffed with mascarpone and truffled olive oil *focaccia farcita al mascarpone con olio tartufato* 52

wafer-thin focaccia with rosemary and sea salt *focaccina sottilissima al rosmarino e sale marino* 36

truffled pizza with smoked prosciutto and slivered arugula *pizza con speck, rucola ed olio tartufato* 38

pizza with diced fresh tomatoes, oregano, and shaved pecorino *pizza con pomodori freschi, origano e pecorino a scaglie* 40

black and white pizza *pizza nera e bianca* 44

wafer-thin focaccia with rosemary and sea salt

focaccina sottilissima al rosmarino e sale marino /// SERVES 4

FOR THE DOUGH

3½ cups bread flour, plus extra
for the work surface (I suggest
Sir Lancelot High-Gluten Bread
Flour from King Arthur Flour
Company; see Mail-Order
Sources, page 183)

1 teaspoon instant yeast

2 teaspoons salt

About 1¼ cups warm water
(110°F.)

5 teaspoons extra-virgin olive oil

FOR THE TOPPING

¼ cup extra-virgin olive oil

1 teaspoon coarse sea salt

12 rosemary sprigs

cook's note The focaccia dough can
be made up to 1 day ahead; allow it to
almost double in volume at room temperature, then refrigerate for up to
24 hours. The cool temperature in the
refrigerator will slow down the yeast's
activity. Allow the dough to return to
room temperature before shaping and
grilling.

My father loves this focaccia—in fact, whenever we go to our favorite pizzeria in Italy, he orders it as soon as we sit down. The pizzaiolo takes a ball of pizza dough, stretches it into a nearly transparent disk, places it on his peel, douses it with olive oil and coarse sea salt, and bakes it just until it starts to blister and turn brown in the hot oven; if there's fresh rosemary in the kitchen, he adds a few sprigs for flavor. You can try sage, thyme, or oregano instead. When the pizza dough is grilled rather than baked, it acquires a smokier scent and retains a suppler texture.

Make the dough according to the directions on page 40, until the point that it has risen for 1 hour.

Cut the dough into 4 pieces. Shape into 4 balls on a lightly floured surface. Cover and let rest for 15 minutes (this allows the gluten to relax, making stretching easier). Using your hands for a lighter texture, spread and push each ball into a flattened circle about 14 inches in diameter. (If you can stretch it even thinner without tearing it, then do so.) Rub or brush both sides of the dough circles lightly with the remaining 4 teaspoons of olive oil.

Heat a grill to a high flame.

Transfer 1 piece of dough at a time directly to the grill. Cook for 1 minute, or until the bottom is very lightly browned and just starting to dry. Using long tongs, flip the dough over.

Top the dough: Using a long-handled brush, brush the top with 1 tablespoon of the olive oil, spreading it almost all the way to the edges. Sprinkle with ¼ teaspoon of the coarse sea salt. Top with 3 of the rosemary sprigs.

Cook the focaccia for 1 to 2 minutes more, or until the bottom crust is crisp and browned. Continue in the same manner with the remaining ingredients. Serve the focaccia hot, warm, or at room temperature. (It is at its best hot off the grill.)

a grain of salt **Until somewhat recently, salt was a very costly ingredient, used parsimoniously in cooking by those who could afford it. The very word *salary* finds its origins in the fact that workers were often paid for their labor in salt. Major roads were built at the time of the ancient Romans to transport salt across the empire. One such road, which still runs right in front of my father-in-law's family home near Ascoli Piceno, is the Via Salaria, which ran from Rome through the Apennines on the Adriatic coast: Stretching more than 150 miles, this was the route by which the Sabines came to fetch salt from the marshes at the mouth of the Tiber River. Sea salt remains the favorite salt in Italy, and today, as in the days of classical Rome, the most important salt flats in Italy are in Sicily and Sardinia: As the sea water evaporates, hills of white salt are left behind, ready to be harvested, packaged, and sold around the world.**

truffled pizza with smoked prosciutto and slivered arugula

pizza con speck, rucola ed olio tartufato /// SERVES 4

FOR THE DOUGH

3½ cups bread flour, plus extra
   for the work surface (I suggest
   Sir Lancelot High-Gluten Bread
   Flour from King Arthur Flour
   Company; see Mail-Order
   Sources, page 183)

1 teaspoon instant yeast

2 teaspoons salt

About 1¼ cups warm water
   (110°F.)

5 teaspoons extra-virgin olive oil

FOR THE TOPPING

1 cup canned chopped Italian
   plum tomatoes (preferably San
   Marzano)

1 cup mascarpone (preferably
   imported Italian)

½ teaspoon salt

¼ cup white truffle olive oil

16 paper-thin slices of speck

2 bunches of arugula, washed,
   dried, stems removed, and cut
   into a chiffonade (see page 98)

½ teaspoon freshly ground black
   pepper

This is my favorite pizza in the world . . . and I eat a lot of pizza. The sauce is a luxurious combination of buttery mascarpone cheese and diced San Marzano tomatoes (a plum-shaped variety grown near Naples)—and once the pizza is grilled to perfection, I shower it with truffled olive oil and arugula and top it with thin slices of speck (a smoked prosciutto from Trentino–Alto Adige, a northeastern Italian region bordering Austria). Be sure to ask for nearly transparent slices of speck: They should almost melt onto the sauce. If the speck is sliced too thick, its texture will be rubbery rather than delicate.

Make and shape the dough according to the directions on page 40.

Heat a grill to a high flame.

Make the topping: In a bowl, combine the tomatoes, mascarpone, and salt. Transfer 1 piece of dough at a time directly to the grill. Cook 1 minute, or until the bottom is very lightly browned and just starting to dry. Using long tongs, flip the dough over. Working quickly and using a long-handled spoon, top with one quarter of the tomato–mascarpone mixture. Spread the mixture on the dough, leaving about ¼ inch of bare pizza crust exposed around the edges.

Cook the pizza for 2 to 3 minutes, or until the bottom crust is crisp and browned. Remove to a plate. Immediately drizzle with 1 tablespoon of the white truffle oil and top with 4 slices of speck. Shower with one quarter of the arugula and sprinkle with ⅛ teaspoon of the pepper. Serve immediately. Continue in the same manner with the remaining ingredients and serve each pizza as it is ready.

cook's note The pizza dough can be made up to 1 day ahead; allow it to almost double in volume at room temperature, then refrigerate for up to 24 hours. The cool temperature in the refrigerator will slow down the yeast's activity. Allow the dough to return to room temperature before shaping and grilling.

pizza with diced fresh tomatoes, oregano, and shaved pecorino [PHOTOGRAPH ON PAGE 43]

pizza con pomodori freschi, origano e pecorino a scaglie /// SERVES 4

FOR THE DOUGH

3½ cups bread flour, plus extra
    for the work surface (I suggest
    Sir Lancelot High-Gluten Bread
    Flour from King Arthur Flour
    Company; see Mail-Order
    Sources, page 183)

1 teaspoon instant yeast

2 teaspoons salt

About 1¼ cups warm water
    (110°F.)

5 teaspoons extra-virgin olive oil

FOR THE TOPPING

4 ripe beefsteak tomatoes (about
    ½ pound each), peeled and
    cut into ¼-inch dice

2 tablespoons extra-virgin olive
    oil

1 garlic clove, minced

2 tablespoons minced fresh
    oregano

¼ teaspoon salt

¼ teaspoon freshly ground black
    pepper

2 ounces pecorino romano,
    shaved into long, thin strips
    with a vegetable peeler

As with any recipe that calls for very few ingredients, there's no room for error here: Use only ripe, juicy summer tomatoes bursting with flavor. If the only tomatoes you can find are bland, greenhouse specimens, try another recipe rather than shortchange yourself. And if you have some fresh mozzarella on hand, try scattering a few slices under the tomatoes—you'll have a fabulous Pizza Margherita.

Make the dough: Mix the flour, yeast, and salt in a food processor (if your processor comes with a plastic blade, use it rather than the steel blade). With the motor running, add enough of the warm water to make a soft dough that rides the blade. Process for 45 seconds. Add a little more water if the dough is dry or a little flour if it is sticky. The dough should be smooth and supple. Grease a bowl with 1 teaspoon of the olive oil, place the dough in it, shape into a ball, roll in the oil to coat on all sides, and cover with plastic wrap. Let rise at room temperature until doubled, about 1 hour.

Cut the dough into 4 pieces. Shape into 4 balls on a lightly floured surface. Cover and let rest for 15 minutes (this allows the gluten to relax, making stretching easier). Using a rolling pin (or your hands for a lighter texture), roll into 10-inch circles; the edges should be slightly thicker than the center. Brush both sides of the dough circles lightly with the remaining 4 teaspoons of olive oil.

Heat a grill to a high flame.

Make the topping: In a bowl, combine the tomatoes, olive oil, garlic, oregano, salt, and pepper.

Transfer 1 piece of dough at a time directly to the grill. Cook for 1 minute, or until the bottom is very lightly browned and just starting to dry. Using long tongs, flip the dough over. Working quickly and using a long-handled spoon, top with one quarter of the topping. Spread the tomato mixture on the dough, leaving about ¼ inch of bare pizza crust exposed around the edges.

Cook the pizza for 2 to 3 minutes, or until the bottom crust is crisp and browned. Remove to a plate and sprinkle with the pecorino romano. Serve immediately. Continue in the same manner with the remaining ingredients, serving each pizza as it is ready.

cook's note To peel a tomato, you can resort to the usual blanching method (see page 149)—or you can use a serrated vegetable peeler on a raw tomato.

The pizza dough can be made up to 1 day ahead; allow it to almost double in volume at room temperature, then refrigerate for up to 24 hours. The cool temperature in the refrigerator will slow down the yeast's activity. Allow the dough to return to room temperature before shaping and grilling.

pizza before tomatoes **When tomatoes were first introduced in Italy in the sixteenth century, people believed they were poisonous. Tomato plants were grown for ornamental purposes only, and cooks shied away from the fruit itself for more than a hundred years. In the nineteenth century, a Neapolitan cook and cookbook writer, Vincenzo Corrado, published one of the first Italian recipes featuring tomatoes. It was roughly then that Neapolitan cooks started topping their already famous flatbreads with tomatoes, giving rise to pizza as we know it today.**

pizza with diced fresh tomatoes, oregano,
and shaved pecorino [RECIPE PAGES 40–41]

black and white pizza

pizza nera e bianca /// SERVES 4

FOR THE DOUGH

3½ cups bread flour, plus extra
for the work surface (I suggest
Sir Lancelot High-Gluten Bread
Flour from King Arthur Flour
Company; see Mail-Order
Sources, page 183)

1 teaspoon instant yeast

2 teaspoons salt

About 1¼ cups warm water
(110°F.)

5 teaspoons extra-virgin olive oil

FOR THE TOPPING

2 tablespoons extra-virgin
olive oil

½ pound fresh ricotta

4 ounces young goat cheese

⅛ teaspoon Tabasco sauce

½ cup black olive paste

cook's note The pizza dough can
be made up to 1 day ahead; allow it
to almost double in volume at room
temperature, then refrigerate for up to
24 hours. The cool temperature will
slow down the yeast's activity. Allow
the dough to return to room temperature before shaping and grilling.

The topping for this pizza combines creamy, fresh ricotta, young goat cheese,
and a few spoonfuls of black olive paste for a dramatic flavor.

Make the dough according to the directions on page 40, until the
point that it has risen for 1 hour.

Heat a grill to a high flame.

Make the topping: In a bowl, combine the olive oil, ricotta, goat
cheese, and Tabasco sauce.

Transfer 1 piece of dough at a time directly to the grill. Cook for
1 minute, or until the bottom is very lightly browned and just starting
to dry. Using long tongs, flip the dough over. Using a long-handled
spoon, top with one quarter of the ricotta mixture. Working quickly,
spread some of the ricotta mixture on the dough, leaving about
¼ inch of bare pizza crust exposed around the edges. Dollop some
of the black olive paste here and there over the ricotta mixture,
leaving it in distinct mounds.

Cook the pizza for 2 to 3 minutes, or until the bottom crust is
crisp and browned. Remove to a plate and serve immediately. Continue in the same manner with the remaining ingredients, serving
each pizza as it is ready.

a yeast primer There can be no risen bread without yeast. Yeast is a living organism that extracts oxygen from sugars in flour to produce carbon dioxide and alcohol when it comes into contact with water. The gases that form are then released, creating gas bubbles in the dough and making the dough rise: the first, miraculous step in making bread, focaccia, and pizza.

In the past, people had to rely on wild yeasts in the air or on homemade yeast starters to make leavened bread. Unless you intend to make your own yeast starter (which is satisfying, but also quite tricky and time-consuming to maintain), you can use one of three forms of commercial yeast: instant, active dry (also known as rapid-rise), or compressed cake yeast. Instant and active dry yeast are minute granules of dried yeast; instant yeast is tinier and slightly more potent than active dry yeast. But the main difference between instant and active dry yeast is that instant yeast can be added directly to flour, whereas active dry yeast needs to be dissolved in warm liquid before it is combined with flour (keep this in mind if you are substituting active dry yeast for the instant yeast I call for in the recipes in this book). Compressed cake yeast, which is sold in a block in the refrigerated section of supermarkets, also needs to be dissolved in warm liquid before it is mixed with flour.

Instant, active dry, and compressed cake yeast vary in potency (the most powerful is instant, followed by active dry, and finally compressed cake yeast), so I suggest you adjust quantities of yeast in a given recipe if you substitute one type of yeast for another: 1 cube of compressed cake yeast, which weighs 0.6 ounces, is equivalent in potency to $2\frac{1}{2}$ teaspoons of active dry yeast and 2 teaspoons of instant yeast. Purchase yeast from a reputable source to be certain it is fresh: If the yeast is dead, the dough won't rise no matter how good your recipe is or how skillfully you knead, shape, and bake (or grill) the bread. To order instant yeast and other baking supplies, see Mail-Order Sources (page 183).

When working with yeast, keep in mind that yeast is temperature-dependent: It falls asleep (becomes inactive) in extremely cold temperatures, speeds up in moderate temperatures, and dies in extremely hot temperatures. Use warm, but not hot, water or liquid when mixing a yeasted dough: 110°F. is just right, activating the yeast without running the risk of scalding it and killing it (use an instant-read thermometer to be sure). Yeast produces carbon dioxide faster in warmer temperatures. As a result, yeasted dough rises more slowly in the refrigerator than at room temperature or near the pilot light of the oven. Slow rises in low temperatures result in bread or pizza with more character; in practical terms, this means that you can make a batch of dough, refrigerate it overnight, and bake (or grill) it the next day.

grilled polenta coins with creamy gorgonzola sauce

polenta alla griglia con salsa al gorgonzola /// SERVES 4

FOR THE POLENTA

¼ teaspoon salt

1½ cups Italian polenta
(preferably coarse stone-
ground)

2 tablespoons extra-virgin olive
oil, plus extra for greasing the
baking sheet

FOR THE GORGONZOLA SAUCE

½ pound gorgonzola dolce, rind
removed, cut into ½-inch cubes

2 tablespoons (¼ stick) unsalted
butter

½ cup heavy cream

⅓ cup freshly grated parmigiano-
reggiano

¼ teaspoon freshly ground black
pepper

cook's note I learned to cook polenta
the old-fashioned way, from my mother:
stirring constantly with a wooden
spoon for 45 minutes. Then one day, I
watched my friend Biba Caggiano
make polenta using a method that was
a total revelation to me: steaming the
polenta in a double boiler. Try Biba's
method, and you'll never find making
polenta drudgery again. Use Italian
coarse stone-ground polenta for a rus-
tic, toothsome texture; see Mail-Order
Sources (page 183).

When I was little, I was hooked on gorgonzola, a nutty blue cheese that has
been produced in Lombardy for centuries. I ate it by the forkful, without bread,
reveling in its aromatic pungency. I still love gorgonzola with or without bread,
and I adore it melted as a sauce for pasta or polenta. In the recipe below, I add
a bit of heavy cream and butter to the gorgonzola to soften its bite, and stir in
grated parmigiano-reggiano to thicken the sauce.

Make the polenta: Bring 6 cups (1½ quarts) of water to a boil in a
heavy 2-quart pot. Add the salt. Pour in the polenta in a thin, steady
stream, beating with a whisk all the while to prevent lumps. In about
5 minutes, when the polenta gurgles and sputters and looks a bit
thicker, somewhat like porridge, transfer it to a clean stainless-steel
or heat-resistant glass bowl. Cover tightly with aluminum foil.

Select a pot whose opening will hold the bowl of polenta perfectly. Pour enough water to come up about 2 inches in the pot. The
bottom of the bowl shouldn't sink too far into the pot (it shouldn't
touch the water), and the bowl should be stable once you've placed
it over the pot.

Bring the water to a gentle boil over medium heat.

Place the bowl with the polenta over the pot of gently boiling
water. Cook over medium-low heat, undisturbed, for 1½ hours. If
the water in the pot is cooking too vigorously, lower the heat
slightly; if the water in the pot is evaporating, add some.

Remove the aluminum foil from the bowl with the polenta. Using
a whisk, beat the polenta until it is creamy and smooth, about
2 minutes. Pour it while still hot onto an oiled 11 × 17-inch baking
sheet, spread it to a thickness of ¼ inch, and smooth the top with
lightly moistened hands. Cool until set.

Meanwhile, make the gorgonzola sauce: Combine all the ingredients in a 1-quart pot. Cook over medium heat, stirring constantly, until the cheeses melt, about 10 minutes. Keep warm over a very low flame. Do not boil or the sauce may curdle.

Cut the cooled and set polenta into rounds with a 3-inch cookie cutter; brush with the olive oil on both sides.

Heat a grill to a high flame.

Grill the polenta until it is golden-brown on both sides but still soft inside, turning once, about 3 minutes per side. Transfer to a platter, arrange it in a single layer, and pour the warm gorgonzola sauce over it. Serve hot.

polenta country I grew up in polenta country. My native city of Milan is surrounded by a lush countryside of cornfields. All across northern Italy, polenta vies with fresh pasta for first place on the table, and often wins. The cooler climate and gentle flatlands that characterize Italy's northern regions have made corn a staple there since it was taken to Europe from America. Corn is grown in yellow and white varieties (the people of the Veneto are especially fond of white cornmeal) and is cooked in myriad ways: as a soft and fluffy mound to accompany rich meat stews; grilled until the outside is charred; baked with bits of cheese or a hearty meat ragù; fried until golden; stirred into bubbling soups; baked into sweet and savory breads; and transformed into heavenly cookies. Leftover polenta is perfect for the grill: just slice it about ¼ inch thick and grill until golden. Serve as a side dish or as a savory base for antipasti.

smoky flatbread

torta sul testo /// MAKES 8 FLATBREADS

3 cups unbleached all-purpose
flour, plus extra for the work
surface
1 teaspoon salt
2 teaspoons baking soda
¾ cup plus 1 tablespoon warm
water

cook's note Never store leftover
bread—or torta sul testo—in the refrigerator: It will harden and dry out. Store
leftover bread at room temperature for
up to 1 day, or freeze in freezer-safe
plastic bags for up to 2 weeks.

This flatbread is a staple in Umbria, where it is served as an accompaniment
to salty cheeses, salt-cured hams, olives, and more. It owes its name to the
testo, a terra-cotta or iron pan with a concave lid in which it was traditionally
cooked. I have found that you can cook a very delicious torta sul testo on a
hot grill: Just watch the flames carefully so that you don't burn the bread. To
keep the bread warm as you finish grilling, wrap it in a clean kitchen towel.

Place the flour, salt, and baking soda in a bowl and mix with a
wooden spoon. Stir in the water. Turn out onto a work surface and
knead for 5 minutes, or until a soft, smooth dough forms, sprinkling
in additional water if the dough is dry or additional flour if it is sticky.
Shape into a flat disk, dust lightly with flour, wrap, and let rest for
30 minutes.

On a very lightly floured work surface, shape the dough into a
2-inch-thick log (it will be about 16 inches long). Cut the dough into
8 equal pieces.

Using a rolling pin, roll out each piece into a 5-inch circle. Prick
each circle 3 times with a fork; this will prevent ballooning as the
flatbreads cook. Arrange the dough circles on very lightly floured
trays in a single layer (try not to stack the dough circles, or they
might stick together).

Heat a grill to a high flame.

Cook as many flatbreads as will fit on the grill until browned on
the bottom, about 2 minutes. Turn and cook until speckled on the
other side, about 2 minutes, then remove to a towel and wrap
to keep warm. Continue grilling in the same manner with the
remaining flatbreads.

Serve hot, warm, or at room temperature. The flatbreads are delicious split in half horizontally (not easy to do, but worth the trouble) and stuffed with freshly grated pecorino romano, ground black pepper, some minced rosemary, and a drizzle of extra-virgin olive oil.

from stone breads to bakeries

It seems impossible: a world without bread. And yet bread is a relatively recent addition to the human diet. When people discovered fire, they started cooking whatever they could catch on the hunt over the live flames. Later, they cooked soups and porridges made of various grains in suspended vessels or on burning hot stones they heated on the fire. Then one day, a bit of porridge fell from the cooking vessel onto a hot stone—and the result was the first flatbread in history. The Egyptians developed ovens—large conical structures much like today's tandoori ovens—that they used for baking bread. The ancient Romans were skilled bakers, and they learned much of their art from the Greeks; they passed their knowledge down from generation to generation, formed active bakers' guilds, and devised steam injection for their ovens to produce crisp-crusted loaves. Many flatbreads baked around the world today are direct descendants of the very first stone breads—fragrant reminders that we all share a common past.

neapolitan calzone

calzone alla napoletana /// SERVES 4

FOR THE DOUGH

3½ cups bread flour, plus extra
for the work surface (I suggest
Sir Lancelot High-Gluten Bread
Flour from King Arthur Flour
Company; see Mail-Order
Sources, page 183)

1 teaspoon instant yeast

2 teaspoons salt

About 1¼ cups warm water
(110°F.)

1 teaspoon extra-virgin olive oil

FOR THE FILLING

⅔ pound fresh whole-milk ricotta

¼ teaspoon freshly ground black
pepper

½ pound thinly sliced prosciutto
cotto or spicy salami, such as
soppressata

4 teaspoons extra-virgin olive oil

Calzone is many things in an Italian kitchen: a round pie, a pizza folded over itself in a half-moon shape, a crunchy fritter filled with all manner of goodies. The unifying feature of all calzoni is that they are stuffed. I love calzoni both baked and fried—and, ever since I started experimenting with focaccia and pizza on the grill, I love them grilled too. You can add 1 tablespoon of chopped fresh sage leaves along with the flour, yeast, and salt in the food processor before activating the motor; the sage will imbue the dough with a lovely herbal flavor, and the dough will be prettily flecked with green.

Make the dough according to the directions on page 40, until the point that it has risen for 1 hour.

Cut the dough into 4 pieces. Shape into 4 balls on a very lightly floured surface. Cover and let rest for 15 minutes (this allows the gluten to relax, making stretching easier). Working with one piece of dough at a time and using a rolling pin, roll each ball out into a 12-inch circle.

Heat a grill to a high flame.

Fill the calzoni: Top half of one circle with one quarter of the ricotta, spreading it gently to the edges with the back of a spoon (do not apply too much pressure or the dough will stick to the work surface and you will have trouble lifting the calzone later). Sprinkle with a pinch of the pepper. Scatter one quarter of the prosciutto or salami over the cheese. Fold the dough over to enclose the filling, creating a half-moon. Press the tines of a fork along the edges of the calzone to seal. Lift the calzone to a very lightly floured tray. Brush the top with ½ teaspoon of the olive oil; flip over; and brush the other side with ½ teaspoon of the olive oil.

Shape the remaining calzoni in the same manner.

Transfer the calzoni to the grill. Cook for 1 minute, or until the bottom is very lightly browned and just starting to dry. Using long tongs, flip the calzoni over.

Cook for 1 to 2 minutes more, or until the other side is also crisp and browned and the dough is cooked all the way through. Serve hot.

cook's note The dough can be made up to 1 day ahead; allow it to almost double in volume at room temperature, then refrigerate for up to 24 hours. The cool temperature in the refrigerator will slow down the yeast's activity. Allow the dough to return to room temperature before shaping.

Be sure to fill and transfer the calzoni to the grill quickly, so the filling doesn't have time to make the dough soggy, or it will stick to the work surface and become impossible to lift without tearing. Use ricotta as long as it's fairly dry and compact (buy it in a cheese shop or specialty market), or opt for fresh mozzarella, grating it and setting it in a colander for 30 minutes to drain before using.

focaccia stuffed with mascarpone and truffled olive oil

focaccia farcita al mascarpone con olio tartufato /// SERVES 8

FOR THE DOUGH

3½ cups unbleached all-purpose
  flour, plus extra for the work
  surface

1 teaspoon instant yeast

2 teaspoons salt

¾ cup warm water (110°F.)

1 tablespoon plus 1 teaspoon
  extra-virgin olive oil

FOR THE FILLING

½ pound mascarpone (preferably
  imported Italian)

2 tablespoons white truffle
  olive oil

½ teaspoon salt

cook's note The focaccia dough can
be made up to 1 day ahead; allow it
to almost double in volume at room
temperature, then refrigerate for up to
24 hours. The cool temperature will
slow down the yeast's activity. Allow
the dough to return to room temperature before shaping and grilling.

The haunting aroma of truffles permeates this positively elegant focaccia. I like to cut it into triangular wedges and serve it as finger food before a formal dinner party. You can make miniature round focaccias if you prefer by shaping the dough into 2-inch circles instead; the recipe below will yield about 24 miniature focaccias.

Make the dough according to the directions on page 40, adding 1 tablespoon of olive oil to the dough, until the point that it has risen for 1 hour.

On a lightly floured work surface, divide the dough into 4 pieces. With your fingers, pat and stretch each piece into an 8-inch circle. Arrange the dough circles on a lightly floured tray in a single layer (try not to stack them or they might stick together). These are the focacce.

Heat a grill to a high flame.

Cook the focacce on the grill until speckled on the bottom, about 2 minutes. Turn and cook until speckled on the other side, about 2 minutes, then remove to a clean tray. Allow the focacce to cool to room temperature.

Using a sharp serrated knife, slit each focaccia in half horizontally. Don't worry if the focaccia tears in spots: It will be delicious nonetheless. (I usually place my left hand flat on top of the focaccia as I run the knife through the focaccia with my right hand; a little pressure usually helps prevent tears.)

Fill the focacce: Spread the mascarpone evenly over the bottom half of each focaccia, and flip the top half over to enclose. Brush both sides of each focaccia with the white truffle oil and sprinkle lightly with the salt.

To serve, return the filled focacce to the grill. Cook for 2 minutes, turning once, or until the mascarpone begins to melt and the outside becomes slightly golden. Serve hot, cut into wedges.

beyond tiramisù: cooking with mascarpone **Mascarpone, a full-fat, creamy cow's-milk cheese from Lombardy, is most often associated with tiramisù in North America. But in Italy, we use it in savory dishes too: We fold it into pasta sauces at the last moment to lend a creamy quality, blend it with smoked salmon as a simple topping for crostini, dollop it onto pizzas that emerge from a blazing oven, and the list goes on and on. Italians think of mascarpone the way Americans think of cream cheese. If you've never tried mascarpone, look for an imported Italian brand rather than a domestic version: Made without additives or guar gum, it has a deep, buttery flavor with just a hint of tanginess. Mascarpone will keep in the refrigerator in its tightly sealed container for a few weeks; once opened, it should be consumed within a week.**

fish and seafood

skewered mussels with pancetta and bread crumbs *spiedini di cozze con pancetta e pangrattato all'aglio* 56

sea bream with caramelized lemons and fresh bay leaves *orata con limoni caramellati ed alloro* 58

herb-crusted tuna steak with arugula and cherry tomato salad *tonno alle erbe aromatiche con insalatina di rucola e pomodorini* 60

monkfish in garlic–lemon bath *pescatrice con limone ed aglio* 61

whole trout with garlicky bread-crumb stuffing *trote farcite al pangrattato ed aglio* 64

tarragon-rubbed salmon *salmone al dragoncello* 66

"buttoned" grouper stuffed with provolone and garlic *cernia abbottonata con provolone ed aglio* 68

sea scallops with tri-color pepper medley and slivered basil *capesante con peperoni arancioni, rossi e gialli e basilico tagliuzzato* 71

stuffed squid *calamaretti ripieni* 72

baby octopus with caper marinade *polipetti con salsina ai capperi* 73

clams in a packet with oregano, garlic, and white wine *vongole al cartoccio all'origano, aglio e vino bianco* 74

herbed shrimp threaded on rosemary skewers *spiedini di gamberi al rosmarino* 76

swordfish bundles with sicilian orange and pine nut stuffing *pesce spada alla siciliana con arance e pinoli* 77

lobster, lemon, and mint salad *insalata di aragosta con limone e menta* 79

smoky seafood salad over shaved fennel *insalata di frutti di mare con finocchio* 80

skewered mussels with pancetta and bread crumbs

spiedini di cozze con pancetta e pangrattato all'aglio /// SERVES 4

2 pounds mussels

2 tablespoons plus ½ teaspoon salt

⅔ cup fresh bread crumbs

2 tablespoons minced Italian parsley

2 garlic cloves, minced

¼ teaspoon freshly ground black pepper

½ pound country bread, cut into 1-inch cubes

¼ pound thinly sliced pancetta

¼ cup extra-virgin olive oil

cook's note In Italy, cooks often shell mussels a crudo (raw), but I find cooking them in a pot for just a minute or two doesn't make them any tougher, and simplifies the procedure tremendously.

The salty flavor of pancetta marries beautifully with the mussels' brininess in this festive dish. If you are especially fond of scallops, try them instead of mussels for a more elegant presentation and sweeter flavor.

If using wooden skewers, soak 4 skewers in water to cover for 30 minutes. Drain.

Meanwhile, cover the mussels with cool water and 2 tablespoons of the salt and refrigerate for 30 minutes. Lift them out of the soaking water, being careful not to disturb the sediment at the bottom of the bowl, and rinse thoroughly in a colander. Scrub the mussels and remove any beards.

Place the mussels in a deep 2-quart pot and cook over medium heat, covered, just until the shells start to open, about 2 minutes (the mussels will not be fully cooked at this point). Uncover and remove from the heat. Cool to room temperature and shell. Discard any unopened mussels.

Heat a grill to a medium-high flame.

In a bowl, combine the bread crumbs, parsley, garlic, the remaining ½ teaspoon of salt, and the pepper.

Roll the mussels in the bread crumb mixture (there will be some left over; reserve it). Thread a cube of bread, a slice of pancetta folded in quarters, and a mussel onto a skewer; repeat, filling up the skewer. Make 4 skewers this way. (There may be some bread or pancetta left over.)

Stir the olive oil into the reserved bread crumb mixture. Roll the skewers in the bread crumb mixture, coating well on all sides, pressing so the mixture adheres.

Cook the mussel skewers on the grill until the bread is golden and the pancetta is cooked, about 5 minutes, turning often to cook evenly. Serve hot.

preparing mussels for cooking

Buy mussels the same day you plan to cook them. Select only tightly closed mussels in the store, and keep them thoroughly chilled until you get home. If the seafood market is far from home, have the fishmonger place a few ice packs in your bag along with the mussels. Once home, rinse the mussels and store in a bowl in the refrigerator, covered with a wet towel. When you are ready to cook the mussels, transfer them to a large bowl and cover with cool water, adding plenty of salt (about $1/4$ cup of salt per quart of water). Soak the mussels for 30 minutes in the refrigerator to purge sand and sediment. Remove the mussels from the salted water using your hands like rakes in order not to disturb the sandy sediment at the bottom of the bowl, and rinse the mussels a few times. Scrub with a stiff brush to get rid of barnacles and clinging grit. Pull off any beards (the thin, tough tufts of hair that protrude from the shell) by tugging firmly with your thumb and forefinger. Check that all mussels are still closed: Tap any gaping mussels gently. If they close within 30 seconds, they are alive (mussels should be alive before cooking and dead after cooking). Discard any unresponsive open mussels. Cook cleaned mussels no more than 1 hour after debearding them, or they might die before they are subjected to heat. After cooking, mussels should open—an indication that they were alive before cooking and an assurance that they are now dead. Any unopened mussels should be discarded, as they were likely dead long before they reached the heat.

sea bream with caramelized lemons and fresh bay leaves

orata con limoni caramellati ed alloro /// SERVES 4

1½ pounds boneless and
   skinless sea bream fillets,
   halved lengthwise and cut into
   16 equal pieces
4 garlic cloves, minced
4 small shallots, minced
3 tablespoons minced oregano
2 large lemons, each cut into
   8 thin slices
16 fresh bay leaves
¼ cup extra-virgin olive oil
1¼ teaspoons salt
¼ teaspoon freshly ground black
   pepper

cook's note Sea bream is one of Italy's great fish. Sweet, moist, not at all fishy, it cooks up beautifully on the grill. Substitute with red snapper.

Cooking chunks of fresh lemon on a hot grill caramelizes them, bringing out their sweetness more than their acidity. You can try limes or oranges instead for a different flavor. To offer guests at a barbecue an original palate cleanser, simply thread chunks of lemons, limes, and oranges on skewers and grill until caramelized, then pass the skewers around like lollipops between courses.

If using wooden skewers, soak 4 skewers in water to cover for 30 minutes; drain.

Place the sea bream fillets with the side that was touching the skin facing up. Sprinkle with the garlic, shallots, and oregano. Roll each fillet into a tight bundle. Thread the bundles onto the skewers, alternating them with the lemon slices and bay leaves; keep them rather close together so the bundles don't unravel. Drizzle the bundles with the olive oil and season with the salt.

Heat a grill to a high flame.

Cook the skewers until the sea bream is firm to the touch and opaque all the way through, turning every minute or so to cook evenly, about 7 minutes total. Serve hot, sprinkled with the pepper.

grilling fish and seafood on skewers Skewering small fish and seafood before grilling makes the job of turning, and therefore of cooking evenly, much easier, and the presentation itself is very festive. You can use decorative metal skewers, wooden skewers, even thick rosemary sprigs or lemongrass stalks to skewer your food for the grill. If using metal skewers, keep in mind that they get really hot, so be careful when turning them! If using wooden skewers, soak them in water to cover for 30 minutes prior to using and, to reduce flare-ups, wrap any exposed part in aluminum foil before placing skewers on the grill. To try your hand at rosemary skewers, select the thickest rosemary sprigs around (see page 76 for more); and for lemongrass skewers (hardly Italian, but delicious!), discard some of the fibrous outer layers before threading the food onto the stalks.

herb-crusted tuna steak with arugula and cherry tomato salad

tonno alle erbe aromatiche con insalatina di rucola e pomodorini /// SERVES 6

3 garlic cloves, minced

2 tablespoons Spice Rub for Fish
and Seafood (page 156)

1¼ teaspoons salt

¼ teaspoon freshly ground black
pepper

6 tablespoons extra-virgin
olive oil

Two 1-pound tuna steaks (about
1 inch thick), skin off

2 bunches of arugula, washed,
dried, and stems removed (see
Note)

20 cherry tomatoes, quartered

½ cup black olives, pitted and
coarsely chopped

Grated zest of 1 large lemon

1 lemon, cut into wedges

cook's note Arugula leaves are
delightfully peppery and pair perfectly
with robust fish like tuna and swordfish. Arugula stems, on the other hand,
are quite bitter, and should be discarded; see page 32 for directions.

Grilled beef is often topped with julienned arugula in Tuscany. In this lighter recipe, tuna is rubbed with dried herbs and spices (oregano, paprika, black pepper, and tarragon), then grilled and served topped with a refreshing arugula salad.

In a shallow container or on a plate, combine the garlic, dry rub, ½ teaspoon of the salt, the pepper, and 3 tablespoons of the olive oil. Rub the tuna steaks in the mixture, coating both sides well. (This can be done up to 2 hours ahead. Refrigerate the tuna until needed.)

Heat a grill to a high flame.

Grill the tuna 3 minutes per side, turning once, for rare; grill longer for medium or well-done tuna (Italians would never serve rare or medium tuna; see below). Remove the tuna to a cutting board, cut on the diagonal into thin slices, and arrange on a serving platter. Sprinkle the top with ¼ teaspoon of the salt.

In a large bowl, toss the arugula, cherry tomatoes, olives, and lemon zest with the remaining 3 tablespoons of olive oil and the remaining ½ teaspoon of salt. Mound over the sliced tuna on the platter, allowing some of the tuna to peek out under the arugula, and serve, decorated with the lemon wedges.

the raw and the cooked In clas-sical Italian cooking, we either cook fish until it is well done or leave it alone and serve it raw. We prepare carpaccio (paper-thin slices of raw fish, usually drizzled with lemon juice and olive oil and served with a sprin-kling of fresh herbs or greens), savor raw sea urchin on the fishing boats with nothing more than a sprinkle of salt, and indulge in raw mussels and oysters. But fish steaks and fillets get cooked all the way through, and a rare piece of fish is considered improperly cooked.

monkfish in garlic–lemon bath

pescatrice con limone ed aglio /// SERVES 4

2 pounds boneless and skinless
   monkfish fillet, purple
   membrane removed, cut into
   3-inch pieces

1¼ teaspoons salt

¼ teaspoon freshly ground black
   pepper

¼ teaspoon dried red pepper
   flakes

5 garlic cloves, 1 minced and
   4 slivered

6 tablespoons extra-virgin
   olive oil

6 tablespoons fresh lemon juice

cook's note Be sure to ask the fishmonger to remove the thin purple membrane that covers the monkfish. As the monkfish cooks, the membrane contracts, making an otherwise tender cut of fish chewy and tough—much like silverskin does to a perfect piece of veal loin.

Called "poor man's lobster," monkfish is firm and sweet and lends itself perfectly to grilling. I like to serve this monkfish surrounded by crisp, emerald spinach leaves for contrast in color and texture, and scatter a julienne of brilliant red peppers around the platter for visual effect. The monkfish tastes best after it marinates for a day or two in the refrigerator, so this is a great make-ahead dish.

Heat a grill to a medium-high flame.

Place the monkfish in a shallow dish; season it on all sides with ½ teaspoon of the salt, ⅛ teaspoon of the pepper, the dried red pepper flakes, and the minced (not slivered) garlic. Drizzle with 1 tablespoon of the olive oil.

Grill 3 minutes per side, turning once, or until the monkfish is firm to the touch and the juices run clear when the monkfish is pierced. Remove to a deep serving platter.

In a bowl, combine the remaining 5 tablespoons of olive oil, the lemon juice, the remaining ¾ teaspoon of salt and ⅛ teaspoon of pepper, and the slivered garlic; pour over the monkfish and set aside to marinate for 1 hour at room temperature or up to 2 days in the refrigerator, turning the monkfish in the marinade once in a while. Serve at room temperature, adjusting the seasoning if needed.

gauging when fish is cooked
The first, and most telltale, sign of doneness is firmness. As fish cooks, it goes from soft to firm; when overcooked, fish becomes hard or flaky. Another clue is opacity: As fish cooks, it changes from translucent to opaque. Finally, with whole fish, look for flesh that lightly pulls away from the bone when a paring knife is inserted into the back of the fish. Don't cook fish until it becomes flaky—that's a sign that you've gone too far.

Ingredients for *monkfish in garlic-lemon bath* [RECIPE PAGE 61]

whole trout with garlicky bread-crumb stuffing

trote farcite al pangrattato ed aglio /// SERVES 4

¼ cup fresh lemon juice

¼ cup plus 2 tablespoons
extra-virgin olive oil

½ cup fresh bread crumbs

4 garlic cloves, minced

1 cup Italian parsley leaves
minced

2 rosemary sprigs, leaves only,
minced

¾ teaspoon salt

¼ teaspoon freshly ground black
pepper

2 whole trout (1 pound each),
gutted, scaled, rinsed, and
blotted thoroughly dry

cook's note If you can get your hands on salmon trout, it works fabulously in this recipe.

Umbria, a landlocked region south of Tuscany, offers a delicious array of fresh-water fish recipes. Trout from the Nera River are especially prized, and are often grilled with a savory stuffing of fresh herbs and bread crumbs, as below. Because the bread crumbs are moistened with quite a bit of olive oil and lemon juice, they form what resembles a savory bread stuffing inside the trout. To make your own bread crumbs, which are more flavorful than store-bought, see sidebar on page 113.

Heat a grill to a high flame.

In a bowl, combine the lemon juice, ¼ cup of the olive oil, the bread crumbs, garlic, parsley, rosemary, ½ teaspoon of the salt, and the pepper. Stuff the cavity of each trout with the mixture. Brush the outside of the trout with the remaining 2 tablespoons of olive oil and sprinkle with the remaining ¼ teaspoon of salt.

If you are using a wire cage or grilling basket for your fish, place the trout in the cage or basket. If not, simply place the trout on the grill.

Cook the trout until the bottom is nicely browned, about 5 minutes. Turn the trout; if the trout is not in a cage or basket, turn very carefully using two long spatulas to prevent the skin from sticking to the grill. Cook until the trout is done all the way through, the bottom is also nicely browned, and the fish feels firm to the touch, about 5 more minutes (or 10 minutes total per inch of thickness at the thickest part).

Remove to a serving platter and enjoy hot.

tips for grilling whole fish large and small In general, I do not advocate buying specialized equipment for cooking only one or two dishes: I find it wasteful and inefficient in terms of kitchen storage (especially in my tiny New York City kitchen). But when it comes to grilling whole fish, the potential problem posed by the fish sticking to the grill is annoying enough to warrant bending the rules. If you grill whole fish fairly often, you might want to buy a wire cage, which prevents direct contact between the fish and the grill so sticking won't be an issue. Here are a few tips to keep in mind when grilling whole fish:

1. Oily fish such as sardines, mackerel, anchovies, tuna, and salmon are ideal choices for the grill, since their higher oil content helps prevent them from sticking.

2. Smaller fish require higher heat, and larger fish lower heat. If the heat is too low for small fish, they will dry out before the outside gets crisp, and if the heat is too high for large fish, the outside will be scorched by the time the inside is cooked through.

3. If you are using a live-fire grill, place smaller fish on the grate directly over the coals, larger fish on a grate farther away from the coals (the thicker the fish, the longer it will take to cook through and the farther away from the coals it should be placed).

4. Turn whole fish only once. The more times you turn fish, the more chances you run of the skin sticking to the grill. The side that touched the grill first will probably be the prettiest, so present your fish accordingly.

5. Lightly brush the fish with oil before placing it on the grill. The grill too should be lightly oiled to prevent sticking.

6. If you don't have a wire cage for grilling whole fish, you may not want to scale the fish before grilling it; the scales will help reduce sticking. This is especially important for delicate, nonoily fish such as red snapper, sea bass, and porgy.

7. If you grill small fish such as sardines on a regular basis, try a square grilling basket (made up of two square grills joined by a hinge); it eliminates the need to slide a spatula under the fish in order to turn it.

8. Small fish can also be threaded in rows on skewers; this won't prevent sticking but will make turning a large number of fish more efficient. When skewering small fish individually, thread each fish through two skewers, arranging the skewers perpendicularly to the body of the fish at the head and tail (if you thread each fish on a single skewer, it will be hard to turn the fish later, as you might find that the fish spins around on the skewer).

tarragon-rubbed salmon

salmone al dragoncello /// SERVES 6

1 cup tightly packed tarragon
  leaves, chopped
1¼ teaspoons salt
½ teaspoon freshly ground black
  pepper
Grated zest of 1 large lemon
¼ cup extra-virgin olive oil
6 boneless salmon fillets
  (½ pound each, 1 inch thick),
  skin on
¼ cup fresh lemon juice

cook's note If you prefer dill to tarragon, this is a perfect recipe in which
to use it.

The combination of tarragon and salmon seems magical to me, especially when a bit of grated lemon zest is added. I love the vibrancy of the three colors—bright green, deep orange, and bold yellow—before cooking, and their more subdued beauty after the salmon is grilled.

In a bowl, combine the tarragon, salt, ¼ teaspoon of the pepper, the lemon zest, and the olive oil. Rub the outside of the salmon fillets with the tarragon mixture, coating well on all sides except the skin side.

Heat a grill to a high flame.

Place the salmon fillets on the grill, skin side up. Cook 2 minutes, or until nicely golden on the bottom. Turn the fillets and cook on the left side until golden, about 2 minutes. Turn to cook on the right side until golden, about 2 more minutes. Finally, turn to cook on the skin side for 1 more minute, or until the salmon is cooked all the way through; it should be firm and no longer translucent when it is done. Remove to a platter, skin side down.

Pour the lemon juice over the salmon, sprinkle with the remaining ¼ teaspoon of pepper, and serve hot.

knowing when fish is fresh

The single most important factor when cooking fish (whether grilled, poached, sautéed, or cooked any other way) is freshness. If fish isn't fresh, there is nothing you can do to make it taste great. Search out a well-stocked, impeccably clean fish store in your city, befriend the fishmonger, and let him or her guide you when making your purchases. Don't be shy: Ask which fish is fresher, which just came in, which was never frozen, which was frozen only once. (The truth is, most fish is sold to wholesalers frozen; it is frozen on the boats immediately after it is caught, then defrosted before it is sold in stores. Some fish is frozen whole, then defrosted, cut into steaks or fillets, and frozen again. This is the fish you want to avoid, for it will cook up dry and flavorless.) If you go to the store with a hankering for monkfish, but the monkfish is of dubious freshness and the red snapper is looking perky, then cook snapper instead. You may need to change the recipe somewhat, but you will undoubtedly be rewarded with a better result. It's easier to tell if fish is fresh when buying whole fish rather than fillets or steaks, so I often buy whole fish and ask the fishmonger to cut it if my recipe calls for it.

The telltale signs of freshness for whole fish are:
- Shiny, sparkling fish with no slimy coating
- Clear, protruding eyes
- Firm flesh (poke the fish; your finger shouldn't leave an imprint)
- Straight tail
- Red gills without any white slime (brown gills mean the blood is oxidizing)
- Tightly adhering scales
- No odor, or a bright, clean ocean scent (saltwater fish) or pond scent (freshwater fish)

With fillets and steaks, discerning freshness is a bit more challenging. Here are the signs to look for:
- Shiny surface with no slime or film
- Translucent appearance (opacity indicates old fish or fish that was improperly frozen)
- Dense grain (avoid fish with spaces or gaps in the flake)
- Firm flesh (again, poke the fish; your finger shouldn't leave an imprint)
- No odor, or a bright, clean ocean scent (saltwater fish) or pond scent (freshwater fish)

"buttoned" grouper stuffed with provolone and garlic

cernia abbottonata con provolone ed aglio /// SERVES 4

1 medium whole grouper (about
    4 pounds), gutted and scaled
2 ounces provolone cheese,
    coarsely grated
2 tablespoons minced Italian
    parsley
1/2 teaspoon salt
1/4 teaspoon freshly ground black
    pepper
4 garlic cloves, minced
1/2 cup fresh lemon juice
1/4 cup extra-virgin olive oil
2 tablespoons water
1 thick, long-stemmed oregano
    branch

cook's note Provolone is a classic
Sicilian cheese. I prefer an aged provolone here, because its sharper flavor
will marry especially well with the garlic's pronounced taste. If grouper is
unavailable, try black sea bass instead.

In Sicily, the technique used here to stuff the fish is known as abbottonata, meaning "buttoned"—because the stuffing is pushed inside small round incisions made along the length of the fish, resulting in a dotted look as though the fish had buttons running down its side. After the fish is cooked, it's nearly impossible to see where the "buttons" are, but you'll be able to taste them when you bite down on a piece with cheese stuffing. If you want more than a hint of cheese, fill the belly of the grouper with a double quantity of provolone stuffing instead of inserting the mixture into incisions, or buttons, along the fish.

Heat a grill to a medium-high flame.

Using the tip of a small paring knife, make eight 1/4-inch-wide × 1/4-inch-deep × 3/4-inch-long slits along each side of the grouper (these will be the "buttons").

In a small bowl, combine the provolone, parsley, 1/4 teaspoon of the salt, 1/8 teaspoon of the pepper, and three quarters of the minced garlic. Push the provolone mixture deep into the incisions you made, making sure it is safely tucked inside and won't fall out during cooking; compact it with your finger and push as much filling inside the incisions as possible.

In another bowl, combine the lemon juice, olive oil, and water with the remaining garlic, 1/4 teaspoon of salt, and 1/8 teaspoon of pepper. Using the oregano sprig, brush some of the mixture on both sides of the grouper.

If you are using a wire cage or grilling basket for your fish, place the grouper in the cage or basket. If not, simply place the grouper on the grill.

Cook the grouper until the bottom is nicely browned, brushing often with the oregano branch dipped in the lemon juice–olive oil mixture. Turn the grouper; if the grouper is not in a cage or basket, turn very carefully using two long spatulas to prevent the skin from sticking to the grill. Cook, brushing with the oregano sprig often, until the grouper is done all the way through and the bottom is also nicely browned and feels firm to the touch, about 10 minutes total per inch of thickness at the thickest part.

Remove to a serving platter and enjoy hot.

why italian parsley? **All the recipes in this book that call for parsley specify Italian parsley. Also known as flat-leaf parsley, this variety has a much more intense herbal flavor than the curly type. It is readily found at specialty markets and greengrocers. Its pointed leaves vaguely resemble those of cilantro, but they are sturdier and darker green, and of course the flavor is completely different. The stems are bitter and must be discarded (although they are great for lending flavor to stocks). Always rinse parsley thoroughly, as the leaves trap quite a bit of grit, then blot dry before using.**

sea scallops with tri-color pepper medley and slivered basil

capesante con peperoni arancioni, rossi e gialli e basilico tagliuzzato ///

SERVES 4

3 tablespoons extra-virgin olive oil

2 garlic cloves, minced

Grated zest of 1 large lime

$^1/_2$ red bell pepper, cut into long, thin strips

$^1/_2$ yellow bell pepper, cut into long, thin strips

$^1/_2$ orange bell pepper, cut into long, thin strips

$^1/_2$ medium purple onion, cut into long, thin strips

1 teaspoon salt

$^1/_4$ cup packed basil leaves, cut into a chiffonade (see page 98)

2 tablespoons cracked black pepper

2 pounds large sea scallops, rinsed and blotted dry

2 tablespoons fresh lime juice

$^1/_4$ cup packed mint leaves, cut into a chiffonade (see page 98)

cook's note Cut the basil and mint leaves into long, thin strips (called chiffonade) just before using them. If you cut them ahead of time, they will turn brown and lose aroma.

These scallops are quite spicy, thanks to an abundant dose of cracked black pepper. They can be served as an elegant appetizer (in that case, the recipe will serve 8), or as a satisfying main course. Choose scallops with a subtle orange hue if possible; they are the females, and taste sweeter than the white (male) ones.

Heat 2 tablespoons of the olive oil in a 12-inch skillet over a medium-high flame. Add the garlic and lime zest and cook for 30 seconds, stirring, or until the garlic releases its aroma. Fold in the red, yellow, and orange peppers and the onion and cook for 4 minutes, or until the vegetables are wilted but still somewhat crunchy. Stir in $^1/_4$ teaspoon of the salt and the basil and cook for 30 seconds more; spoon onto 4 plates.

Combine the cracked pepper and the remaining $^3/_4$ teaspoon of salt on a plate. Dip the scallops in the remaining tablespoon of olive oil, then in the salt and pepper mixture, coating both sides well and pressing to make the salt and pepper mixture adhere.

Heat a grill to a high flame.

Cook the scallops on the hot grill until browned on both sides and cooked all the way through, turning once, about 4 minutes total; remove to a plate.

Arrange the scallops over the cooked pepper mixture and serve hot, sprinkled with the lime juice and mint.

stuffed squid

calamaretti ripieni /// SERVES 4

1 cup fresh bread crumbs

2 small garlic cloves, very finely minced

1 cup Italian parsley leaves, minced

1/2 cup salted capers, rinsed and chopped

1/4 teaspoon freshly ground black pepper

1/4 cup whole milk

1 pound small squid bodies, cleaned

2 tablespoons extra-virgin olive oil

1/8 teaspoon salt

1 recipe Light Tomato Sauce (page 149) or lemon wedges

cook's note For the most tender texture, look for the smallest squid possible. Cuttlefish can be cooked the same way, but they are generally chewier than squid.

Squid—calamari in Italian—are a favorite seafood all over Italy. They are braised, sautéed, fried, and, of course, grilled by home cooks and restaurant chefs alike, typically flavored with little more than garlic, parsley, and olive oil. This recipe is a classic from home kitchens across southern Italy; a bread crumb stuffing laced with plenty of capers offers a delightful counterpoint to a delicate tomato sauce or a squeeze of fresh lemon juice.

In a bowl, combine the bread crumbs, garlic, parsley, capers, and pepper. Stir in the milk.

Using a tiny spoon, stuff the mixture into the squid. Don't over-stuff the squid or they may burst on the grill. There might be leftover stuffing. Close the opening of each squid with a toothpick, spearing it diagonally. Brush the squid with the olive oil and season the outside with the salt. (The squid can be prepared up to 12 hours ahead and refrigerated until you are ready to grill.)

Heat a grill to a high flame.

Grill the squid until it is opaque and lightly browned on the outside, 3 to 5 minutes, turning as needed. Do not overcook or the squid will be tough and chewy. (The cooking time will be determined by how high the flame is and how far the squid is from the flame.)

Remove the squid to a cutting board and discard the toothpicks. Cut on the bias into 1/2-inch-thick slices. If using the tomato sauce, heat it to a light simmer. Serve the squid hot, on a pool of tomato sauce, or pass lemon wedges around the table instead.

baby octopus with caper marinade

polipetti con salsina ai capperi /// SERVES 4

¼ cup plus 2 tablespoons
   extra-virgin olive oil

2 tablespoons white-wine vinegar
   or fresh lemon juice

1 garlic clove, peeled

¼ cup salted capers, rinsed

12 basil leaves

¼ teaspoon salt

¼ teaspoon freshly ground black-
   pepper

⅛ teaspoon dried red pepper-
   flakes

½ red bell pepper, cut into long,
   thin strips

Peel of 1 zucchini, cut into long,
   thin strips (see Note)

2 scallions, white parts only,
   thinly sliced on the diagonal

1½ pounds baby octopus,
   beaks removed, rinsed and
   blotted dry

cook's note To remove only the dark green peel from zucchini, use a vegetable peeler. The peel stays delightfully crunchy even after marinating with the other ingredients, because it's much less watery than zucchini flesh; reserve the zucchini flesh for other dishes (pasta sauces, risotto, or even grilled vegetable kebabs).

If you're a bit squeamish when it comes to octopus, this might just be the dish to turn you around. Baby octopus are much more tender than large ones, and they absorb the flavor of the marinade better—and the fact that their tentacles are barely 1 inch long makes them easier on the eyes than large octopus. You will find baby octopus at Italian, Portuguese, Greek, and Spanish fish markets, or order them from the Mail-Order Sources (page 183). If you like, try squid grilled the same way: The tentacles are especially delicious tossed with this vivacious caper sauce.

Heat a grill to a high flame.

Meanwhile, in a blender or food processor, combine ¼ cup of the olive oil with the vinegar, garlic, capers, basil, salt, pepper, and red pepper flakes until nearly smooth. Pour into a large bowl and add the red bell pepper, zucchini peel, and scallions.

Toss the baby octopus with the remaining 2 tablespoons of the olive oil in a large bowl. Cook on the hot grill until it is firm all the way through and opaque, about 10 minutes total, turning as needed to cook evenly. Remove to the bowl with the caper marinade and the vegetables. Toss to coat well and serve hot, warm, or at room temperature, adjusting the salt if needed.

clams in a packet with oregano, garlic, and white wine

vongole al cartoccio all'origano, aglio e vino bianco /// SERVES 4

4 pounds littleneck clams

2 tablespoons plus 1¼ teaspoons salt

⅓ cup extra-virgin olive oil

2 garlic cloves, minced

¼ cup minced Italian parsley

¼ cup minced oregano

½ cup dry white wine

6 ripe plum or 3 ripe beefsteak tomatoes, peeled, seeded, and diced (see page 149)

¼ teaspoon freshly ground black pepper

cook's note Use small clams, preferably littlenecks, for the most tender texture, as larger clams can be chewy. If cockles are available, use them instead: Their delicate texture and taste more closely resembles that of Italian clams (vongole), which are subtly briny in flavor, sweet, and small, about half the size of littlenecks.

The flavor of this classic clam dish is defined by a generous dose of white wine and parsley. You can toss the clams and their cooking juices with freshly cooked linguine or spaghetti, shell them and spoon them atop grilled bread rubbed with garlic, or simply enjoy them as is, dipping the opened shells into the savory sauce before indulging in each mouthful.

Soak the clams in cool water to cover with 2 tablespoons of the salt for 30 minutes. Lift them out of the soaking water, being careful not to disturb the sediment at the bottom of the bowl, and rinse thoroughly in a colander.

Heat a grill to a medium-high flame.

In a bowl, combine the olive oil, garlic, parsley, oregano, wine, tomatoes, the remaining 1¼ teaspoons salt, and the pepper.

Cut sturdy aluminum foil into four 12-inch squares. Place on a work surface, shiny side up.

Pile one quarter of the drained clams on one side of each sheet of aluminum foil and spoon one quarter of the wine and tomato mixture over each portion. Fold the free side of the foil over to enclose the clam and tomato mixture; seal the short sides of the foil first, then the long side. Seal the edges well or the tomato mixture may leak out and flare up on the grill.

Place the foil packets on the hot grill, seam side up, and cook for 8 minutes, or until the clams open fully. Bring the packets to the table and let guests open their own.

herbed shrimp threaded on rosemary skewers

spiedini di gamberi al rosmarino /// SERVES 4

¼ cup fresh lemon juice

¼ cup extra-virgin olive oil

1 garlic clove, minced

½ cup fresh bread crumbs

3 tablespoons freshly grated
  caciocavallo or parmigiano-
  reggiano

1 teaspoon salt

⅛ teaspoon freshly ground black
  pepper

2 tablespoons minced Italian
  parsley

1½ pounds large shrimp, shelled
  and deveined

¼ pound country bread, cut into
  1-inch cubes

24 long-stemmed rosemary
  skewers, stripped of the
  bottom 2 inches of leaves
  (see Note)

cook's note I often use rosemary sprigs as skewers for seafood and delicate meats like veal and chicken. Select rosemary with thick, almost branch-like stems for the best results: As the skewers cook, the rosemary will exude its intense aroma and perfume the shrimp. I usually strip the leaves off the bottom 2 inches of the sprigs to create sturdier skewers and to make threading food easier.

Combining fish or seafood with cheese, as in this recipe, is common in southern Italy, Sicily, and Sardinia. I enjoyed a similar dish in Calabria years ago, and I loved the way the cheesy bread crumbs clung to the grilled shrimp.

Heat a grill to a high flame.

On a rimmed plate, combine the lemon juice, olive oil, and garlic.

On another plate, combine the bread crumbs, caciocavallo, salt, pepper, and parsley.

Dip the shrimp and bread in the lemon juice mixture, then roll in the bread-crumb mixture, coating well on all sides. There will be some bread-crumb mixture left over.

Thread the shrimp and bread cubes onto the rosemary skewers, alternating them. You will probably be able to thread 2 shrimp and 2 bread cubes on each skewer.

Grill until golden brown on all sides, about 3 minutes per side, turning once. The shrimp will feel firm to the touch and no longer be translucent when they are ready. Serve hot.

cooking fish steaks and fillets: a primer In general, fish steaks are preferable to fillets on the grill, especially when they are at least ½ inch thick. Thicker steaks take longer to cook through, so they develop a delicious, rich, smoky flavor and a crispy crust before they overcook. Keep the skin on fillets and steaks to seal in moisture and help diminish the risk of sticking. Score the skin a few times with shallow diagonal cuts before placing the fish on the grill. Also, be sure the skin is lightly oiled before grilling to reduce the risk of sticking. If the skin sticks, don't panic: Carefully lift the fish with spatulas and serve it with the side that was stuck face down on the plate.

swordfish bundles with sicilian orange and pine nut stuffing

pesce spada alla siciliana con arance e pinoli /// SERVES 4

1 cup packed crumbled crustless white bread

$1/2$ cup freshly grated pecorino siciliano or pecorino romano

$1/4$ cup minced Italian parsley

$1/4$ cup sultana raisins (see Note)

$1/4$ cup pine nuts

$1/16$ teaspoon ground cinnamon

$1/4$ cup fresh lemon juice

$1/3$ cup plus 2 tablespoons fresh orange juice

$1/4$ cup extra-virgin olive oil

1 teaspoon salt

$1/4$ teaspoon freshly ground black pepper

$1 1/4$ pounds swordfish steak

8 fresh bay leaves

cook's note If the raisins are really dry, soak them in warm water to cover for 15 minutes, drain, and then use in the stuffing as directed.

In this traditional Sicilian preparation, slices of swordfish are pounded thin with a meat mallet, then topped with a mixture of pine nuts, raisins, grated pecorino, and bread plumped in freshly squeezed orange juice before they are rolled into bundles and grilled to succulent perfection. The sweet flavor of the stuffing and the use of pine nuts and raisins hark back to Arab occupation of Sicily. Don't overdo it on the cinnamon in the stuffing, though, or the fish may just end up tasting like candy.

If using wooden skewers, soak 8 skewers in water to cover for 30 minutes; drain.

In a bowl, combine the bread, pecorino, parsley, raisins, pine nuts, cinnamon, 3 tablespoons of the lemon juice, $1/3$ cup of the orange juice, the olive oil, salt, and pepper.

Cut the swordfish into $1/4$-inch-thick slices. You should have 16. One by one, place the swordfish slices between sheets of wax paper and pound with a meat mallet until they are about $1/8$ inch thick, being careful not to tear them.

Top each of the slices with some of the pine nut and orange mixture and roll into tight bundles to enclose. Don't worry if some of the stuffing falls out; it's bound to. Spear 2 bundles on each skewer, placing a bay leaf between them.

Heat a grill to a high flame.

In a bowl, mix the remaining tablespoon of lemon juice and 2 tablespoons of orange juice.

Grill the skewers, turning often and brushing with the lemon and orange juice, until the swordfish is cooked all the way through and evenly browned on all sides, about 5 minutes total. Serve hot.

lobster, lemon, and mint salad

insalata di aragosta con limone e menta /// SERVES 4

²/₃ cup plus ¼ cup extra-virgin
    olive oil

½ cup fresh lemon juice

2 garlic cloves, thinly sliced

1 medium purple onion, cut into
    long, thin strips

1½ cups packed mint leaves,
    cut into a chiffonade (see
    page 98)

1½ teaspoons salt

¾ teaspoon freshly ground black
    pepper

8 medium lobsters (about 1½
    pounds each), split in half
    lengthwise through the back
    and tail

cook's note If you don't want to kill the lobster yourself, ask the fishmonger to do it for you. But either way, be sure to grill the split lobster a maximum of 4 hours after it's been killed.

The flavors of this spectacular salad are distinctly Sardinian: The succulence of grilled lobster chunks mingles with the vibrancy of lemon and the freshness of mint. Although some cooks advocate grilling lobster claws, I find that by the time they are cooked through, the tail meat has turned to rubber. So save your lobster claws for boiling, and grill only the halved tails.

Heat a grill to a high flame.

In a large serving bowl, combine ²/₃ cup of the olive oil, the lemon juice, garlic, onion, mint, salt, and pepper.

Separate the lobsters' tail sections from the heads and claws. (Reserve the claws for boiling and the lobster heads for stock.) Brush the flesh side of the split lobster tails with the remaining ¼ cup of olive oil. Place the lobster tails, flesh side down, on the grill. Cook until the flesh turns pink and is firm to the touch, about 4 minutes. Turn and cook on the shell side for 4 more minutes, or until the shell is entirely pink and the lobster is cooked all the way through. The lobster flesh should be firm and no longer shiny.

Remove the lobster tails to a cutting board. Scoop out the flesh from the shells and cut into 1-inch chunks. Toss the lobster chunks with the lemon-mint dressing and adjust the seasoning if needed. Serve hot, warm, or at room temperature.

sardinia's lobster coasts

Sardinia is renowned for its lobsters. But unlike American lobsters, which have huge front claws, Mediterranean lobsters more closely resemble spiny lobsters. They have small claws (similar to shrimp claws) and only the tail meat is eaten.

Sardinians typically cook lobster in the simplest ways possible, to highlight its subtle flavor. They split it and grill it over live coals or boil it until its flesh is tender and pink. Sauces are just as simple: Extra-virgin olive oil and a squeeze of lemon juice are the most common condiments, perhaps flavored with a hint of mint or parsley; salsa corallina features these ingredients plus tomatoes and the lobster's coral; and Catalan-style lobster is served with a sweet-and-sour sauce of oranges, lemons, tomatoes, bay leaves, and oregano, a specialty of Alghero.

smoky seafood salad over shaved fennel

insalata di frutti di mare con finocchio /// SERVES 6

½ pound mussels

2 tablespoons plus ¾ teaspoon
salt

½ pound cockles

¼ cup plus 3 tablespoons extra-
virgin olive oil

¼ cup fresh lemon juice

1 teaspoon Dijon mustard

¼ teaspoon freshly ground black
pepper

2 tablespoons minced Italian
parsley

1 garlic clove, minced

1 pound large shrimp, shelled
and deveined

1 pound small squid bodies,
cleaned

2 small or 1 medium fennel bulb,
trimmed, quartered, cored, and
sliced paper-thin

cook's note Instead of the fennel,
you can add steamed new potatoes
and string beans to this seafood salad
to transform it into a hearty summer
main course.

Seafood salads abound in Italy. Every region with a coastline boasts its own version: tossed with arugula, with sliced fennel, orange slices, olives. . . . But the seafood is almost always poached, rarely grilled. And while I love the delicate flavor of poached seafood, particularly lobster and shrimp, I have a particular fondness for grilled seafood salads. The smokiness of the seafood offsets the lemony dressing perfectly, and the result is absolutely magical. The key to a great seafood salad, as I learned from my mother, is to toss the still-hot seafood with the lemony dressing. The seafood is much more permeable when warm, and the flavors of the dressing penetrate more deeply, creating an intensely flavored salad.

Soak the mussels in cool water to cover with 1 tablespoon of the salt for 30 minutes. In another bowl, soak the cockles in cool water to cover with 1 tablespoon of the salt for 30 minutes. Lift the mussels and cockles out of the soaking water, being careful not to disturb the sediment at the bottom of the bowl, and rinse thoroughly in a colander. Scrub the mussels and remove any beards.

Heat a grill to a medium-high flame.

Meanwhile, in a small bowl, whisk together ¼ cup of the olive oil, the lemon juice, mustard, ½ teaspoon of the salt, the pepper, parsley, and garlic.

Cut a sturdy sheet of aluminum foil into a 12-inch square. Place the aluminum foil, shiny side up, on a work surface. Pile the cockles and mussels on one side of the foil and fold the free side of the foil over to enclose; seal the short sides of the foil first, then the long side. Seal the edges well.

Place the foil packet on the hot grill, seam side up, and cook for 8 minutes, or until the cockles and mussels open fully. Open the packet, strain the cooking juices through a cheesecloth-lined sieve, and stir into the prepared mustard dressing. Shell half of the cockles and mussels. Remove the shelled mussels and cockles, and those still in the shell, to a bowl. Discard any unopened mussels and cockles.

Toss the shrimp and squid with 1 tablespoon of the olive oil. Cook on the hot grill until they become firm and opaque, about 2 minutes per side for the shrimp and 45 seconds per side for the squid, turning once. Don't overcook the squid, or they will be chewy. Remove the grilled shrimp to the bowl with the mussels and cockles. Cut the squid into 1/4-inch-thick rings and add to the bowl as well.

Pour the mustard dressing over the warm seafood mixture in the bowl; toss to coat well and distribute the flavors.

Toss the sliced fennel in a bowl with the remaining 1/4 teaspoon of salt and the remaining 2 tablespoons of olive oil. Arrange on a serving platter. Mound the warm seafood mixture and its dressing over the fennel. Serve warm or at room temperature.

storing fish and seafood after purchase **Fish and seafood are very susceptible to deterioration and must be consumed as soon as possible after purchase. Keep fish and seafood cold (with ice packs or in a cooler bag if necessary) on the way home from the market, because bacteria multiply very quickly at warmer temperatures. Once home, remove your fish and seafood from the original wrapping. Rinse fish and thoroughly blot dry. Half-fill a large colander with ice, place whole fish on it, and cover with more ice, then set the colander over a bowl and refrigerate the fish until you are ready to cook it. Steaks and fillets must be wrapped in clean and dry wax paper before storing on ice in the colander. Seafood such as clams, mussels, shrimp in the shell, and so on should be kept in a bowl in the refrigerator and covered with a towel. Be sure to use fish or seafood within a day of purchase and, above all, keep it cold until you are ready to cook it.**

meat
and poultry

chicken stuffed with fennel and prosciutto

pollo al finocchietto selvatico ripieno di prosciutto /// SERVES 4

½ cup chopped fennel stalks and
    fronds (the celery-like stems
    and dill-like leaves at the top of
    fennel bulbs)
1 tablespoon plus ½ teaspoon
    salt
2 garlic cloves, peeled
¼ pound prosciutto di Parma or
    San Daniele, fat still attached
    (see Note)
1 teaspoon fennel seeds,
    coarsely crushed in a mortar
¼ cup extra-virgin olive oil
4 chicken breast halves
    (¼ pound each), butterflied
¼ teaspoon freshly ground black
    pepper

cook's note Be sure to include some of the delicious, pearly white fat from the prosciutto in the stuffing for the chicken. As the chicken bundles cook, the fat will melt, basting the chicken from the inside and keeping it wonderfully moist.

Marrying wild fennel, prosciutto, and garlic with game or fowl is commonplace in the Marches region, in central Italy. The mixture is most often stuffed inside whole rabbits for the roasting spit, in which case the dish is known as porchetta, and it is one of the Marches' proudest offerings. I adapted this heady stuffing to butterflied chicken breasts, creating lovely bundles that can be sliced on the diagonal after cooking to show off the gorgeous pink filling. Since wild fennel can be hard to find in North America, I substitute some minced fennel fronds and crushed fennel seeds to approximate its flavor.

Bring 1 quart of water to a boil over medium-high heat. Add the fennel stalks and fronds and 1 tablespoon of the salt; cook for 5 minutes. Drain and rinse under cool water to stop the cooking. Drain again, then squeeze dry.

On a cutting board, mince the boiled fennel stalks and fronds, garlic, and prosciutto very fine. Place in a bowl and stir in the fennel seeds and 1 tablespoon of the olive oil.

Place the butterflied chicken breasts on a work surface, smooth side facing down. Scatter the fennel mixture over the breasts. Roll to enclose into tight bundles. Tie with butcher's string. Rub the outside with 1 tablespoon of the olive oil, the remaining ½ teaspoon of salt, and the pepper. Set aside.

Heat a grill to a high flame.

Grill the stuffed chicken breasts until golden brown on all sides and cooked through, about 10 minutes total. Remove to a clean cutting board. Discard the string. Cut on the diagonal into thick slices. Arrange the slices on a platter and serve immediately, drizzled with the remaining 2 tablespoons of olive oil.

tender chicken morsels in rosemary–chili marinade

pollo disossato al rosmarino e peperoncino /// SERVES 6

2½ pounds boneless chicken
legs, skin on

2 lemons, 1 halved and 1 cut into
thin slices

¼ cup extra-virgin olive oil

2 tablespoons minced rosemary

6 garlic cloves, minced

1 teaspoon dried red pepper
flakes

1 teaspoon black peppercorns,
coarsely crushed in a mortar

1½ teaspoons salt

cook's note Boneless chicken legs
are much more tender after grilling
than boneless chicken breasts, and
have a deeper, meatier flavor.

The trio of garlic, rosemary, and dried pepper flakes works wonders on boneless chunks of chicken. I like to marinate the chicken for up to 2 days in the refrigerator if possible; the longer you marinate the meat, the more tender it will become, and the better the flavors of the marinade will penetrate. Before grilling the chicken, return it to room temperature, which will help it cook through more evenly.

Rinse the chicken under cool water, dry it, rub it with 1 of the lemon halves, and place it in a large container. Toss it with the olive oil, rosemary, garlic, red pepper flakes, and black peppercorns; set aside to marinate for 2 hours at room temperature or up to 2 days in the refrigerator.

When you are ready to cook, season the chicken with the salt. Heat a grill to a medium-high flame.

Place the chicken, skin side down, on the grill. Cook until it is browned on the bottom, about 8 minutes. Turn and cook until the chicken is browned on the other side and cooked all the way through, about 8 more minutes.

Arrange the chicken on a serving platter. Sprinkle with the juice from the remaining lemon half and serve hot, garnished with the lemon slices.

pairing herbs and meat To pair herbs and meats, follow your instincts: Whether you add sage or oregano to lamb should depend largely on your personal taste. The only other consideration is one of relative potency: Delicate meats are best suited to delicate herbs, or small amounts of potent herbs; and strongly flavored meats are better with bold herbs, or with a generous dose of milder herbs. Here are a few guidelines to consider:

• Rosemary, thyme, sage, tarragon, oregano, marjoram, and bay leaves are strong. They can overwhelm pork and poultry if used abundantly. They withstand slow cooking, gently releasing aroma into a dish.

• Basil, parsley, chives, chervil, and dill are delicate. They are best with lighter meats. Fold them into finished dishes to maintain their subtle flavor.

brine-salted chicken in spicy marinade and fire-roasted tomato sauce

pollo alla diavola in salamoia con salsa di pomodori alla griglia /// SERVES 4

FOR THE CHICKEN

1 cup kosher salt (this is the
   correct amount!)

4 quarts cool water

2 young roasting chickens (about
   3 pounds each)

1 lemon, halved

¼ cup extra-virgin olive oil

¼ to ½ teaspoon cayenne
   pepper

1 long-stemmed rosemary branch

FOR THE TOMATO SAUCE

2 pounds (4 medium or 3 large)
   ripe beefsteak tomatoes

1 large yellow onion, peel on and
   scored once lengthwise to
   prevent splitting

¼ cup extra-virgin olive oil

¼ teaspoon cayenne pepper

½ teaspoon salt

10 basil leaves, torn

cook's note This tomato sauce is only worth making when fresh, juicy, flavorful tomatoes are available—in other words, in the summer. You can still make a fabulous pollo alla diavola without the roasted tomato sauce; simply serve the chicken with a few lemon wedges for sprinkling at the table.

Pollo alla diavola, or "chicken cooked the devil's way," is standard fare in Italy. A young chicken is split through the backbone and marinated with olive oil and cayenne pepper or freshly ground black pepper, then grilled over live flames. But just how did the reference to the devil become part of the equation? Some say it's because it's devilishly spicy. Others say it's because it's cooked over live flames, like those used to cook devils in hell. Either way, it's delicious. I soak the chicken in a salt brine for 2 days before grilling it to ensure it emerges tender and moist; the difference the salt brine makes is unbelievable. Serve the chicken with a salad of mixed baby greens for a fabulous light lunch.

Make a salt brine by dissolving the salt in the water in a very large pot (the chickens will have to fit inside the pot too, so keep this in mind when selecting the pot). If necessary, add more cool water to keep the chickens entirely submerged.

Rinse the chickens and blot dry. Rub with the lemon halves.

Spatchcock the chickens: Place each chicken on a cutting board with the breast side facing down. Using a sharp knife or pair of kitchen scissors, make a lengthwise cut down one side of the backbone to the tail. Make a second lengthwise cut down the other side of the backbone. Remove and discard the backbone (or save it for stocks and broths). Flip the chicken around so that it is facing breast side up. Cut the wing tips off. Spread the chicken open like a book. With a meat mallet, smash the chicken gently a few times to crack the bones in its rib cage and breast, flattening it out; this will help it cook through faster and more evenly on the grill. If you like, you can make a small incision where the legs meet the breast and tuck the leg knuckles in the incisions to give the chicken a tidier appearance.

recipe continues

Add the chickens to the pot with the salt brine and turn once or twice in the salt brine; cover and refrigerate for 48 hours. Remove from the brine, rinse thoroughly, and blot dry. Place on a large tray.

If using a charcoal grill, pile the coals on either side of the grill, place a drip pan in the center underneath the grate, and heat the grill to high. If using a gas grill, build a three-zone fire: turn one burner on high, another on medium, and a third on low.

Make the tomato sauce: Grill the tomatoes and the whole onion until charred all over and very soft, about 25 minutes over the coals of a charcoal grill or the high flame on a gas grill, turning to cook evenly. The tomato flesh should be falling apart and the skins should be sticking to the grill; if not, the tomatoes won't have a sufficiently smoky flavor.

Peel the tomatoes and slip off the skin and the outer layer of the onion. Finely chop the tomatoes and the onion and transfer to a 1-quart pot. Stir in the olive oil, cayenne pepper, and salt. Heat over a medium-high flame for 10 minutes, or until nicely thickened, stirring once in a while. Cool to room temperature and stir in the basil. (The sauce can be made up to 2 days ahead and refrigerated; return to room temperature before serving, adjust the seasoning, and fold in the basil at the last minute.)

preparing poultry the italian way In Italy, cooks rinse poultry in cool running water, then rub it with cut lemon halves. The lemon takes away the poultry's gamy flavor and makes it taste brighter and fresher. The poultry is then blotted dry so when it is cooked it won't steam in its own water. If you don't want the poultry to retain a lemony taste, rinse it in cool water, then blot dry and proceed with your recipe. But no matter how you plan to cook your poultry, always wipe down all counters, sinks, and anything else that came into contact with the raw poultry with bleach or a powerful cleanser, and wash your hands thoroughly with soap.

To finish the chicken, in a small bowl, mix the olive oil and cayenne pepper. Brush the oil–cayenne mixture over the chickens using the rosemary branch and place on the grill, breast side down over the coals of a charcoal grill or the high flame on a gas grill. Cook for 10 minutes, or until the bottom is nicely browned and the skin is crispy, brushing with the oil–cayenne mixture once in a while. Flip the chickens and cook for 10 more minutes, or until the other side is nicely browned.

If using a charcoal grill, move the chickens over the drip pan, close the lid, and grill indirectly until cooked all the way through; if using a gas grill, cook over the medium flame, and move to the low flame if they are browning too quickly. When the chickens are done, the flesh should be firm, no longer pink, and the juices should run clear when the thigh is pierced, about 35 to 45 minutes. (A meat thermometer inserted at the highest part of the thigh should read 180°F.; don't let the thermometer touch bone, though.) If necessary, turn the chickens breast side down again and grill for 2 to 3 more minutes over the coals or high flame, just long enough to crisp up the skin again. Serve hot, with the sauce.

three-meat meatballs with lemony mint pesto

polpette di tre carni con pesto al limone ed alla menta /// SERVES 4

FOR THE MEATBALLS

2 ounces crustless white bread,
   crumbled (3 average slices)
1/2 cup whole milk
1/2 pound coarsely ground pork
1/2 pound coarsely ground veal
1/2 pound coarsely ground beef
1/4 pound ground pork fat
1 large egg
4 garlic cloves, minced
1/2 cup minced Italian parsley
2 teaspoons salt
1/8 teaspoon cayenne pepper

FOR THE MINT PESTO

2 garlic cloves, peeled
2 cups tightly packed mint leaves
1/2 teaspoon salt
1/4 teaspoon freshly ground black
   pepper
3 tablespoons fresh lemon juice
1/2 cup extra-virgin olive oil

cook's note Use fatty, flavorful cuts
to make meatballs. I like pork shoulder
or butt, veal shoulder, and beef chuck.
A bit of added pork fat (or asking the
butcher to grind the pork with quite a
bit of fat still attached) helps the meatballs stay moist. Be sure to ask the
butcher to grind the meat only once
with the coarse plate; this will also ensure moist meatballs.

A combination of ground pork, veal, and beef is used to make these succulent meatballs, and bread plumped in milk is added to provide lightness and body. And while my recipe suggests shaping the meatballs into flattened ovals rather than traditional rounds, you can certainly opt for the latter. I prefer flat-tened ovals because there is more surface area that develops a crisp crust on the grill, much like a grilled burger.

Make the meatballs: In a large bowl, soak the bread in the milk for 5 minutes; squeeze dry. Add the ground pork, veal, beef, pork fat, egg, garlic, parsley, salt, and cayenne pepper, and knead with your hands until smooth and well mixed.

With lightly moistened hands, shape the meat mixture into golf-ball-size pieces. Roll each between your palms into a flattened oval. Set aside on a tray in the refrigerator for up to 24 hours. (The flavor improves if you allow the meatballs to sit for at least a few hours.)

Make the mint pesto: In a very large mortar with a pestle, crush the garlic with the mint, salt, and pepper until a semismooth paste forms. Add the lemon juice and olive oil, beat until combined, and set aside. If your mortar isn't large enough to accommodate all the mint at once, make the pesto in batches, or use a food processor instead. (The pesto can be made up to 2 hours ahead of serving.)

When you are ready to cook, heat a grill to a high flame.

Grill the meatballs in a single layer until they are browned lightly on the outside and cooked all the way through, 5 to 8 minutes total, turning once. Serve hot, drizzled lightly with the mint pesto.

herb-marinated pork chops
over grilled pepper salad

[RECIPE PAGES 92–93]

herb-marinated pork chops over grilled pepper salad

costolette di maiale ai peperoni /// SERVES 4

[PHOTOGRAPH ON PAGE 91]

FOR THE PEPPER SALAD

2 red bell peppers

2 yellow bell peppers

2 orange bell peppers

1 garlic clove, thinly sliced

1 tablespoon minced marjoram

1 tablespoon minced basil

1 tablespoon white-wine vinegar

¼ cup extra-virgin olive oil

½ teaspoon salt

¼ teaspoon freshly ground black
   pepper or ⅛ teaspoon dried
   red pepper flakes

FOR THE PORK CHOPS

4 bone-in pork chops from the
   loin (about ½ pound each)

2 tablespoons extra-virgin
   olive oil

½ teaspoon salt

2 tablespoons Spice Rub for
   Meat and Poultry (page 157)

1 lemon, cut into wedges

cook's note Select thick pork chops on the bone: When meat is grilled on the bone, it has a more intense taste. And there's nothing like holding a juicy chop in your hands and biting it clean!

In Abruzzo, strips of bell peppers are often stirred into simmering chicken, pork, and lamb stews, and this dish is a takeoff on such Abruzzese classics. I love serving grilled meats, particularly pork chops, over grilled peppers marinated with olive oil, basil, marjoram, and garlic: The peppers' sweet flavor balances the smoky meat perfectly. While you can use any color pepper you favor, I prefer orange, yellow, or red peppers (or a mix of all three) and avoid green peppers, which are not quite sweet enough for this dish.

Make the pepper salad: Heat a grill to a high flame.

Grill the peppers, turning every few minutes with tongs to cook evenly, until the skin is blackened all over and the flesh is soft, 15 to 30 minutes. The peppers should be nearly collapsing when done.

Remove to a bowl and cover tightly with aluminum foil. Set aside for 30 minutes; the steam in the covered bowl will help loosen the skin from the flesh of the peppers. Uncover the bowl and slip the skin off the peppers with your fingers. Even if you are tempted to run the peppers under cool water to remove bits of clinging skin, don't do it: You would be rinsing away the delicious smoky flavor. If needed, use a clean towel to wipe away clinging bits of skin from the peppers. Cut the peppers in half, scoop out the seeds, stem, and any membrane, and cut into wide strips. In a clean bowl, toss the pepper strips with the garlic, marjoram, basil, vinegar, olive oil, salt, and pepper. Set aside. (This can be done up to 2 days ahead; refrigerate the peppers until needed and return to room temperature before serving.)

Make the pork chops: Rub the chops with the olive oil, salt, and spice rub, coating well. Set aside for 30 minutes at room temperature (or up to 2 hours in the refrigerator).

Grill the pork chops until browned on one side, about 5 minutes. Turn and grill until browned on the other side and cooked all the way through, about 5 more minutes. The total cooking time will depend on the thickness of the chops, the strength of the flame, and how far the chops are from the flame.

Distribute the pepper salad among 4 plates and use a spoon to spread it to the edges. Place a pork chop on top of the salad on each plate and serve hot, passing the lemon wedges at the table.

a taste for chili The love of spicy food is a feature common to the kitchens of Abruzzo, Molise, Calabria, and Basilicata, where chilies are used both fresh and dried to lend a distinctly spicy note to many of the characteristic dishes. In Abruzzo and Molise, neighboring regions that stretch along the Adriatic coast just north of Apulia, chili is lovingly referred to as diavolicchio, from *diavolo,* meaning "devil," and it is infused in olive oil or lard with slivered garlic as a simple sauce for pasta, stirred into marinades for fish and seafood, and folded into forcemeats for sausages and salami. In Basilicata, prized varieties of peppers are cultivated, including the elongated red peppers from Senise, then dried for use throughout the year in fish soups, tomato or lamb sauces, and vegetable sautés. And in Calabria, hot peppers are incorporated in simmering ragùs, added to homemade sausages, and hung over doorframes along with garlands of garlic. But aside from these regions, most Italians in fact rarely reach for chilies. The North American misconception that Italians typically cook with them arose because most of the Italian immigrants who settled in North America came from impoverished chili-loving regions like Abruzzo, Molise, Calabria, and Basilicata in search of a better life.

savory sausage and sweet grape skewers

spiedini di salsiccia ed uva /// SERVES 4

1½ pounds Italian sausages with
    fennel seeds, casings pierced
    with a fork to prevent bursting

½ pound very large, seedless
    blush or red grapes

Eight 1-inch cubes of country
    bread

2 tablespoons extra-virgin
    olive oil

¼ teaspoon salt

⅛ teaspoon freshly ground black
    pepper

cook's note Check the Mail-Order Sources (page 183) to have fresh Italian sausages shipped to your home.

Combining sausages and grapes may seem strange: The contrast between the sweet and the savory is quite extreme, but it's an ancient Italian custom. Once you taste the two together, you'll be hooked. In my first cookbook, *Rustico: Regional Italian Country Cooking,* I included a recipe that has become a favorite in my cooking classes and on my brunch table: pork sausages sautéed with grapes in a veil of olive oil. I love the flavors of this easy dish so much that I adapted it to the grill, and the result is magical. Be sure to select large, juicy grapes for the skewers, so they don't wither over the flames; and seek out a good Italian butcher who makes fresh sausages on a regular basis. When a dish calls for as few ingredients as this one, only impeccable products will do.

If using wooden skewers, soak 8 skewers in water to cover for 30 minutes; drain.

Heat a grill to a medium-high flame.

Grill the sausages until they are golden brown on all sides, turning often, about 12 minutes total. The sausages will not be cooked all the way through at this point; they should need about 4 more minutes of cooking. Remove to a cutting board and, using a sharp knife, cut into 1-inch pieces on the diagonal. (If the grapes are small, cut the sausages into smaller pieces so they both cook through at the same time.)

Thread the pieces of sausage and the grapes onto each of 8 skewers, alternating them. Finish each skewer with 1 cube of bread. Place on a tray. Drizzle with the olive oil, sprinkle with the salt and pepper, and return to the hot grill.

Grill, turning to cook evenly, until the sausages are cooked all the way through, the grapes are soft but not mushy, and the bread is golden, about 4 minutes. Serve hot.

"the birds that ran away" (veal and pancetta skewers)

uccellini scappati /// SERVES 4

1 recipe polenta (see Note)

1½ pounds veal butt or veal top round, cut into ¼-inch-thick scaloppine and pounded thin with a mallet

1 bunch of sage leaves

16 thin slices pancetta (about ¼ pound), plus ¼ pound pancetta, cut into ½-inch cubes

2 tablespoons (¼ stick) unsalted butter, melted

½ teaspoon salt

¼ teaspoon freshly ground black pepper

cook's note To cook polenta the easy way (without stirring constantly for 45 minutes), use the double-boiler method on page 46.

Until a few decades ago, one of Lombardy's most characteristic dishes was polenta e osei ("polenta with little birds"): songbirds such as thrush or lark skewered with pancetta and sage, then cooked on the spit and served in a mound over a bed of polenta shaped to resemble a bird's nest. Cooking osei (Milanese dialect for uccelli, or birds) is now banned in Italy, so people devised other ways to satisfy their appetite for this traditional dish—by substituting quail for the songbirds or, as here, by using veal or pork instead. That's how this dish got its name: The birds literally "ran away." Butter rather than olive oil is brushed on the veal as it grills, since there is little olive cultivation in Lombardy (see sidebar). Serve the bundles atop a mountain of steaming polenta for the most authentic experience.

Make the polenta as directed on page 46 and keep it covered in the bowl set over a pot of simmering water until you are ready to serve the meat.

If you are using wooden skewers, soak 8 skewers in water to cover for 30 minutes; drain.

Heat a grill to a medium-high flame.

Cut the scaloppine into a total of 16 equal pieces. Spread the scaloppine on a work surface in a single layer. Top each with 1 sage leaf and 1 thin slice of pancetta. Roll each into a tight bundle.

Skewer the bundles and the remaining ingredients in this order: 1 sage leaf, 1 bundle, 2 pancetta cubes, 1 sage leaf, 1 bundle, and so on, repeating the procedure until all the ingredients are skewered. Brush the bundles with the melted butter, and sprinkle with the salt and pepper on all sides.

Grill the skewers, turning to cook evenly, until the bundles are golden brown all over and cooked and the pancetta cubes have rendered their fat and are cooked all the way through, about 8 minutes total.

When the skewers are ready, remove the bowl of polenta from the pot of simmering water and adjust the salt if needed. Whisk vigorously to make sure the polenta is lump-free. Pour onto a wooden board, marble slab, or large platter.

Remove the bundles and pancetta from the skewers. Mound over the polenta and serve immediately.

lake garda's golden olive oil

Nestled in the north of Italy close to Switzerland, Lombardy is a region where cows graze in fertile flatlands, lush valleys, and imposing mountains, making for a wonderful array of cheeses and a generous hand with butter and cream in the kitchen. Olive trees cannot survive Lombardy's cold winters, so butter has typically been the fat of choice for cooking—except around the shores of Lake Garda, Italy's largest lake, where a favorable microclimate created by pre-Alpine lakes has allowed the cultivation of olive trees at the highest latitude in the world. Lake Garda's extra-virgin olive oil is one of Italy's proud DOP (Denomination of Protected Origin) products, made using primarily Casaliva, Frantoio, Leccino, and Pendolino olives. It has a maximum of 0.6 percent acidity, a color ranging from green to yellow, a moderately fruity scent, and bitter, peppery, and almond tones. To sample this unique olive oil, check the Mail-Order Sources (page 183).

florentine steak topped with slivered arugula

bistecca alla fiorentina con rucola /// SERVES 4

4 T-bone steaks (1 inch thick)

¼ cup extra-virgin olive oil, plus extra for passing at the table

1 teaspoon salt

½ teaspoon freshly ground black pepper

2 bunches of arugula, washed, dried, and cut into a chiffonade (see sidebar)

cook's note If you want to make the classic tagliata di manzo, buy 4 boneless rib-eye steaks instead of the T-bones, grill them as below, and slice on the diagonal before topping with the arugula.

Florence is famous for its bistecca alla fiorentina, an imposing T-bone that averages around one inch of thickness. The meat is brushed liberally with fruity olive oil and grilled over an open fire, then seasoned with nothing more than salt the moment it is removed from the grill. Another famous Tuscan dish is tagliata di manzo, or sliced steak, typically served very rare topped with a shower of slivered arugula. This recipe combines the best of both worlds: a juicy T-bone grilled to perfection topped with fragrant arugula. Select a fruity, peppery extra-virgin olive oil to stand up to the steak's robust flavor.

Heat a grill to a high flame.

Brush the steaks with the olive oil. Grill, turning once, until they are medium-rare, about 4 minutes per side (cook longer if desired). Remove to a platter and season with the salt and pepper.

Top with the arugula and serve immediately, passing additional olive oil at the table.

how to chiffonade arugula and other leafy greens **The term chiffonade refers to fine, long strips of leafy vegetables or herbs. To chiffonade basil, spinach, arugula, or any other green leaf, simply:**

1. Wash and dry the leaves thoroughly.

2. Discard any stems.

3. Stack 4 or 5 leaves on top of one another.

4. Roll the stack of leaves like a cigar.

5. Slice across the roll into thin, long strips with a sharp knife.

Once cut into a chiffonade, herbs and vegetables cannot be stored for long—they lose aroma rapidly and oxidize—so it is best to use the chiffonade within minutes. You can, however, simplify last-minute work by cleaning and stacking the leaves ahead and refrigerating them until you are ready to cut them into a chiffonade.

peppery rosemary-rubbed rib-eye steak

bistecca pepata al rosmarino /// SERVES 4

¼ cup extra-virgin olive oil

¼ cup minced rosemary

1 tablespoon cracked black
    pepper

4 garlic cloves, minced

4 rib-eye steaks (½ pound each if
    boneless, 1 pound each if
    bone-in, about ½ inch thick)

1 teaspoon salt

cook's note Rib-eye steaks come
from the rib portion of the animal and
are among the most prized cuts of
beef. They are extremely tender and
do beautifully on the grill, and their
meaty flavor is perfectly offset by fruity
olive-oil-based marinades such as this
one. Steaks from the rib can be boneless or bone-in; bone-in steaks tend to
be the favorite among true carnivores,
who just can't see eating a steak if
there's no bone to nibble on.

Rosemary works wonders on full-flavored red meats like beef and lamb. One of Italy's most characteristic herbs, it grows wild in the countryside, especially in marshy areas along the coast, into huge, towering bushes with light mauve flowers and a heavenly pine-like scent. It does well inside even in winter, so try growing some at home. You'll be rewarded with fresh rosemary all year long. Rosemary branches are often thrown onto glowing embers in Italy to perfume meat and fish as they grill, and thick sprigs can be used as skewers (see page 76).

Combine the olive oil, rosemary, pepper, and garlic in a shallow dish. Rub the oil mixture on both sides of the rib-eye steaks, coating well. Refrigerate for 2 to 24 hours (the longer you marinate the meat, the stronger the herb flavor will be).

When you are ready to cook, heat a grill to a high flame.

Grill the steaks, turning once, until they are medium-rare, about 4 minutes per side (cook longer if desired).

Serve immediately, sprinkled with the salt.

garlic-studded pork loin with medieval spices

porchetta con spezie medievali /// SERVES 4

6 garlic cloves, peeled

1 1/2 teaspoons salt

3/4 teaspoon freshly ground black pepper

1/8 teaspoon ground cloves

1/8 teaspoon freshly grated nutmeg

1/8 teaspoon ground coriander

2 rosemary sprigs, leaves only

1 boneless pork loin (about 3 pounds), with some fat still on

1/4 cup lard or extra-virgin olive oil

1 cup dry red wine

cooking with wine **The key to selecting wine for cooking is to choose wines that you would happily drink—after all, the wine's essential characteristics will be passed on to the final dish. That being said, don't reach for great vintages or wines that cost a bundle: a good drinking wine is perfect for cooking. I generally consider the dish I am making, pick a wine I would enjoy drinking with it, and then select a similar wine for cooking it—or simply use up last night's bottle of wine.**

This is a grill-friendly version of the spit-roasted suckling pig that has made the town of Arezzo in Tuscany famous. Instead of an entire suckling pig, I use pork loin, but the medieval spices used to flavor the meat (cloves, nutmeg, coriander, and black pepper) remain the same. Brushing the pork loin with red wine as it grills prevents it from drying out and imbues it with a subtly sweet flavor.

In a mortar with a pestle, crush the garlic with 1/2 teaspoon of the salt, 1/4 teaspoon of the pepper, the cloves, nutmeg, coriander, and rosemary leaves until a paste forms.

Using a small paring knife, make about sixteen 1/4-inch-wide × 1 1/4-inch-deep × 3/4-inch-long incisions in the pork loin. Press the spice–rosemary mixture into the incisions using your fingers. If there is any leftover spice mixture, rub it on the outside of the pork loin. Also rub the outside of the pork loin with the lard or olive oil and season it with the remaining teaspoon of salt and 1/2 teaspoon of pepper.

Heat a grill to a medium flame.

Grill the pork loin until it is browned on the outside and cooked all the way through, 30 to 45 minutes, turning to cook evenly and brushing with the red wine using a long-handled brush. When a meat thermometer is inserted, the internal temperature of the pork should read 175°F.

Remove the pork to a cutting board. Cover with aluminum foil and let it rest for 10 minutes. Uncover and cut into thin slices on the diagonal. Serve hot, warm, or at room temperature. A salad of bitter greens such as frisée or endive makes the perfect accompaniment.

baby lamb chops in garlic, green peppercorn, and mustard marinade

costolette di agnello marinate con aglio, pepe verde e senape /// SERVES 4

2 garlic cloves, minced

1 tablespoon green peppercorns, coarsely crushed in a mortar

4 rosemary sprigs, leaves only, minced

6 thyme sprigs, leaves only, minced

Grated zest of 1 large lemon

¼ cup extra-virgin olive oil

¼ cup Dijon mustard

12 baby rib lamb chops, frenched (see Note)

1 teaspoon salt

1 lemon, cut into wedges

cook's note Chops from the rib are most elegant, especially when frenched. Frenched chops have perfectly bare bones, with all the meat, fat, and gristle stripped away for a clean appearance. Butchers will french chops if asked—and it's worth asking them to do it, as the job is laborious and requires a very sharp knife.

This is one of the most popular recipes in my cooking classes in New York. The combination of green peppercorns and Dijon mustard is astoundingly good—and even more so when paired with a flavorful meat like lamb, which does best with intense marinades. I love these chops with the Seared Cabbage Hearts with Toasted Caraway Seeds (page 140).

Combine the garlic, green peppercorns, rosemary, thyme, lemon zest, olive oil, and mustard in a shallow container or on a plate. Rub the lamb chops on both sides with the mixture, pressing with your hands so it adheres. Refrigerate for 2 to 24 hours.

When you are ready to cook, heat a grill to a high flame.

Season the lamb chops with the salt.

Grill the lamb chops until browned on the outside and rosy inside, turning once, about 2 minutes per side; a delicate pink juice should run out when the lamb chops are pierced. (Cook longer for well-done chops.) Serve hot, passing lemon wedges at the table.

sardinian smoked lamb

agnello al mirto /// SERVES 8

12 fresh myrtle branches (see
Note)

1 cup freshly grated pecorino
sardo or pecorino romano
cheese

8 garlic cloves, minced

2 tablespoons minced rosemary

¼ cup packed coarsely chopped
Italian parsley

¾ teaspoon freshly ground black
pepper

3 pounds boneless leg of lamb,
fat still on, butterflied and
lightly pounded with a meat
mallet

2 tablespoons extra-virgin olive
oil, plus extra if desired

1½ teaspoons salt

cook's note You can find myrtle at
most florists in North America, but be
sure to rinse it thoroughly before
using. If myrtle is unavailable, add aromatic wood such as oak to the coals.

Sardinians are masters at grilling over an open fire. They build fires for spit-roasting suckling pig and whole lamb using sturdy sticks, and throw aromatic wood (usually lentisk and juniper wood) into the flames. Myrtle, a bush whose tart purple berries are used to make a bracing liqueur in Sardinia, is often added to firewood, and grilled or poached meats are often wrapped with fresh myrtle branches to acquire a myrtle scent for a day or two before they are sliced and served. Traditionally Italians seldom serve rare lamb (or veal, or fish for that matter), but leg of lamb is much more succulent when it is still a bit pink inside.

If using a charcoal grill, pile the coals on either side of the grill, place a drip pan in the center underneath the grate, and scatter the myrtle branches over the coals. If using a gas grill with a dedicated smoker box, place the myrtle branches in the smoker box; if using a gas grill without a dedicated smoker box or an electric grill, place the myrtle branches on a sheet of aluminum foil, fold into a tightly sealed rectangle, poke a few holes in the foil pouch, and place the pouch directly over a burner under the grate.

Heat the grill to a medium flame.

In a small bowl, combine the pecorino, garlic, rosemary, parsley, and ¼ teaspoon of the pepper. Place the butterflied lamb in front of you, with the smooth side (the one with the fat still attached) on the counter. Spread the garlic–herb mixture over the butterflied lamb and roll tightly to enclose. Rub the outside of the lamb with the olive oil. Season with the salt and the remaining ½ teaspoon of pepper, and tie tightly with butcher's string.

Place the lamb on the grill over the drip pan (if you are using one), close the lid, and cook undisturbed for 1 hour. Uncover the grill (stand back, as there may be quite a bit of smoke) and, using a meat thermometer poked into the highest part, test for doneness: The lamb should read 125°F. for rare, 145°F. for medium-rare, about 160°F. for medium, and 170°F. for well-done. If needed, add more coals (and myrtle branches or a second myrtle smoking pouch) to the fire, and cover the grill to finish cooking the lamb to the desired doneness. The lamb will take anywhere from 1 to 1 1/2 hours, depending on the strength of the flame and the distance of the lamb from the fire.

Remove the lamb to a cutting board. Cover with aluminum foil and let it rest for 10 minutes before carving (otherwise the juices will run out and the lamb will be dry). Uncover the lamb, cut into 1/2-inch-thick slices, and arrange on a platter. Serve hot. If you like, drizzle with additional extra-virgin olive oil.

the mediterranean brush

Italians refer to the plants that grow spontaneously in the countryside and along the coast as "la macchia mediterranea," or "Mediterranean brush." They are the same plants that have thrived across the Mediterranean basin (not just Italy) for thousands of years, and include olive trees, myrtle, lentisk, juniper, rosemary, mint, wild fennel, broom, and oleander. Some are used in cooking and to make wildflower honeys and liqueurs; others are tossed into roaring fires to flavor meat and fish.

mixed grilled skewers

spiedini misti /// SERVES 4

½ pound boneless pork loin, cut into 8 equal cubes (about 2 inches each)

1 tablespoon minced rosemary

½ pound boneless lamb loin, cut into 8 equal cubes (about 2 inches each)

1 tablespoon minced sage

½ pound boneless and skinless chicken breast, cut into 8 equal cubes (about 2 inches each)

1 tablespoon minced thyme

1 red bell pepper, cut into 8 cubes

½ pound slab pancetta, cut into 16 chunks (optional)

1 large yellow onion, cut into 8 chunks

1 green bell pepper, cut into 8 cubes

¼ cup extra-virgin olive oil

½ teaspoon freshly ground black pepper

8 juniper berries, crushed in a mortar

1 teaspoon salt

Mom and Dad's Chili Sauce (page 155)

Here is the classic grigliata mista (mixed grill) of Italy. Regional variations abound, and not all grigliate feature skewered meats like this one. Threading pancetta on the skewers not only lends flavor, it also provides fat, which ensures moister, more succulent meat. I added a trio of vegetables (red and green bell peppers and onions) for a more colorful presentation and sweeter flavor, like my mother always did with her skewers.

If you are using wooden skewers, soak 8 skewers in water to cover for 30 minutes; drain.

Toss the pork with the rosemary, coating both sides well, and set aside. Toss the lamb with the sage, coating both sides well, and set aside. Toss the chicken with the thyme, coating both sides well, and set aside.

Make the skewers: Thread 1 piece of pork, 1 red pepper cube, 1 piece of pancetta (if using), 1 piece of lamb, 1 onion chunk, 1 piece of pancetta, 1 piece of chicken, and 1 cube of green pepper onto each skewer. Place on a tray. Drizzle with the olive oil, sprinkle with the pepper and juniper, and marinate at room temperature for up to 2 hours (or refrigerate for up to 24 hours).

Heat a grill to a high flame.

Season the skewers with the salt. Grill until they are golden brown on all sides, turning often, about 8 minutes total. While the lamb can be rosy inside, the chicken and pork need to be cooked all the way through (they should register 180°F. on a meat thermometer). Serve hot, with Mom and Dad's Chili Sauce on the side.

cook's note In Umbria and Tuscany, pork liver would also be threaded onto the skewers. You can vary the meats used as long as they all cook through in roughly the same amount of time. Avoid tough cuts like shoulder, neck, and butt in favor of delicate, quick-cooking cuts like filet and loin, and your skewers will be delicious.

beef and prosciutto bites with crushed juniper berries

manzo e prosciutto con bacche di ginepro /// SERVES 2 TO 4

1 pound flank steak, cut into 8
    thin slices and pounded with a
    meat mallet

8 juniper berries, finely crushed in
    a mortar

8 thin slices prosciutto di Parma
    or San Daniele

8 sage leaves

1/2 teaspoon salt

1/4 teaspoon freshly ground
    black pepper

2 tablespoons extra-virgin
    olive oil

1 recipe Raw Tomato Sauce
    (page 147)

cook's note I like flank steak for the bundles: Its rich, meaty taste and firm texture stand up to the prosciutto stuffing beautifully. If you prefer a more buttery texture and less pronounced taste, opt for filet mignon instead.

I enjoyed these delicious bundles in Spoleto, a medieval Umbrian town, many years ago. The haunting flavor here comes from juniper berries, which are lightly crushed and sprinkled over the beef before it is rolled into bundles. Juniper berries are about twice the size of peppercorns and have a gorgeous blueish tint; they are used to make gin and to flavor cured hams, preserved cabbage, and other robust foods in northern Italy, where they grow wild in the countryside. Serve the bundles on a bed of sautéed escarole or spinach, accompanied by Raw Tomato Sauce (page 147).

If using wooden skewers, soak 4 skewers in water to cover for 30 minutes; drain.

Place the slices of meat on a work surface in a single layer. Sprinkle evenly with the crushed juniper berries. Top each slice of steak with 1 slice of prosciutto. Roll into tight bundles.

Thread the bundles onto 4 skewers, alternating each bundle with a sage leaf. When threading the bundles onto the skewer, leave a bit of space between them, or the parts that are stuck together will not cook through before the outer parts burn. Sprinkle the skewers with the salt and pepper and drizzle with the olive oil. Set aside at room temperature for 1 hour.

Heat a grill to a high flame.

Grill the skewered bundles until they are golden brown all over, turning to cook evenly, about 5 minutes total. They should still be rosy inside. Serve hot, with the raw tomato sauce.

pounding meat with a mallet
To flatten a slice of meat (or fish) using a meat mallet, sandwich the meat between two sheets of wax paper or plastic wrap. Using the flat side of the mallet, pound the meat until it becomes as thin as you want it. If you don't have a mallet, use the flat side of a chef's knife instead.

rabbit with savory caper sauce

coniglio con salsina ai capperi /// SERVES 2 TO 4

FOR THE RABBIT

1 rabbit (about 3 pounds), cut
   into 8 pieces

1 tablespoon Spice Rub for Meat
   and Poultry (page 157)

3 tablespoons extra-virgin
   olive oil

$\frac{1}{2}$ teaspoon freshly ground black
   pepper

$\frac{1}{2}$ teaspoon salt

FOR THE SAUCE

2 tablespoons salted capers,
   rinsed

1 salted anchovy, boned, gutted,
   and rinsed, or 2 anchovy fillets
   packed in oil, drained

$\frac{1}{4}$ cup packed Italian parsley
   leaves

1 large garlic clove, peeled

$\frac{1}{4}$ teaspoon freshly ground black
   pepper

1 tablespoon white-wine vinegar

$\frac{1}{3}$ cup extra-virgin olive oil

cook's note Should you have access
to hare rather than rabbit, by all means
use it in this succulent recipe. Its
gamier flavor will mate perfectly with
the intense caper sauce.

In this favorite main course from Umbria, chunks of rabbit are brushed with olive oil, and a salty, lightly vinegared sauce of capers, garlic, and anchovies is served alongside. Even if you don't like anchovies, try the sauce: The anchovies melt into it, leaving only a savory note and not the slightest trace of fishiness.

Make the rabbit: Toss the rabbit pieces with the spice rub, olive oil, and pepper. Refrigerate for 2 hours (or up to 2 days).

Heat a grill to a medium-high flame.

Meanwhile, make the sauce: In a blender or food processor, combine the capers, anchovy, parsley, garlic, pepper, and vinegar. Slowly add the olive oil in a thin, steady stream, until the sauce is thick and emulsified.

Season the rabbit with the salt. Grill until browned on the outside and cooked all the way through, 25 to 30 minutes, turning often to ensure even cooking. If the rabbit starts to burn on the outside before the center has a chance to cook through, move it farther away from the flame to a cooler part of the grill. Serve the rabbit hot, with the caper sauce on the side.

vegetables

sausage-stuffed onions and frying peppers

cipolle e peperoni ripieni di salsiccia /// SERVES 6

4 medium yellow onions

1 tablespoon plus ½ teaspoon salt

¼ pound Italian sausage, casings removed and crumbled

¼ cup freshly grated pecorino toscano or pecorino romano

½ cup fresh bread crumbs

1 large egg, beaten to blend

2 garlic cloves, minced

⅓ cup minced Italian parsley

¼ teaspoon freshly ground black pepper

2 tablespoons extra-virgin olive oil

2 frying peppers, halved and seeded

cook's note For a vegetarian version, omit the sausage and add minced rosemary and thyme to the bread-crumb stuffing. Or try a stuffing from Lombardy: Combine ½ cup finely crumbled amaretti (almond macaroons), ¼ cup freshly grated parmigiano-reggiano, 1 egg, a pinch of nutmeg, salt, and pepper.

One of Tuscany's great dishes is baked onions stuffed with sausage, bread crumbs, and pecorino. But why not grill the onions instead, and add some frying peppers (long, thin-skinned peppers) to the mix? Do be careful to cook the sausage stuffing all the way through; if the onions or peppers start to burn on the outside before the sausage has a chance to cook, move them farther from the flame on a charcoal grill or lower the heat on a gas or electric grill.

Bring 2 quarts of water to a boil in a 5-quart pot over high heat. Peel the onions, cutting away the root ends just where they meet the bases of the onions and cutting the stem ends where they meet the tops of the onions, being careful to leave the onions' round shape intact.

Using a teaspoon, scoop out about 3 tablespoons of the flesh from each onion and set aside; be careful not to break the onions as you do this. There should be 2 layers of onion still left intact all around. (Your eyes will likely start to tear as you do this, but these onions are worth crying over.)

Place the onion shells (but not the scooped-out flesh) in the pot of boiling water. Add 1 tablespoon of the salt and cook the onions for 8 to 10 minutes, or until barely tender. Remove with a slotted spoon to a bowl of ice water, drain, place upside down on a plate to remove excess water, and blot dry.

Finely mince the scooped-out onion flesh. Mix thoroughly in a bowl with the sausage, pecorino, bread crumbs, egg, garlic, parsley, the remaining ½ teaspoon of salt, the pepper, and 1 tablespoon of the olive oil.

Arrange the onion shells and the pepper halves on a tray. Fill each with some of the sausage mixture and compact with the back of a spoon or your hand to ensure the filling doesn't fall out. Brush the outsides of the onions and pepper halves with the remaining tablespoon of olive oil.

Heat a grill to a medium-high flame.

Place the onions and pepper halves, stuffing side down, on the grill. Grill for 5 to 10 minutes, or until the sausage is half-cooked and the onions and peppers are lightly browned; be careful not to scorch the stuffing. Turn and cook for 5 to 10 minutes more, or until the sausage is fully cooked; there should be no pink or raw spots left in the sausage. The frying peppers may cook through faster than the onions; remove them from the grill earlier if needed. Serve hot.

homemade bread crumbs

Making fresh bread crumbs is so easy that I never buy packaged bread crumbs. And not only is it easy, it's a great way to use up leftover bread, and homemade bread crumbs taste much better than store-bought. To make your own, slice day-old bread and tear it into a food processor. Activate the motor and stand back: It may take a few minutes to process the bread into fine crumbs, especially if the bread is very dry. You can also make bread crumbs using fresh bread, but they will be moist rather than crunchy. If you make bread crumbs from really dry bread, you should be able to store them in an airtight container for up to 1 month; if you use fresh bread, however, the bread crumbs may become moldy after a few days, so be careful.

zucchini ribbons with dill and slivered almonds

zucchine alla griglia con aneto e mandorle /// SERVES 4

2 medium zucchini (¾ pound
   total), cut lengthwise into
   ¼-inch-thick ribbons
½ teaspoon salt
¼ cup plus 2 tablespoons extra-
   virgin olive oil
½ cup slivered almonds
½ teaspoon paprika
2 to 3 tablespoons fresh lemon-
   juice
¼ teaspoon freshly ground black
   pepper
¼ cup chopped dill

cook's note Watery vegetables like zucchini prefer intense heat. The goal is to ensure they don't steam on the grill and become even more water-logged.

Toasting almonds with paprika certainly is not a traditional Italian technique—in fact, almonds are hardly ever toasted in the Italian kitchen. Pine nuts are often toasted for pesto, and almonds are toasted for cookies and cakes, but toasted almonds are rarely incorporated in savory dishes. No matter: The flavor is lovely, pure, and simple, and beautifully offsets the lemony marinade for the zucchini.

Heat a grill to a high flame.

Toss the zucchini with ¼ teaspoon of the salt and 1 tablespoon of the olive oil.

Grill the zucchini until browned lightly on the outside and crisp-tender, about 3 minutes per side, turning once. Remove to a platter.

Heat 1 tablespoon of the olive oil in an 8-inch skillet over a medium flame. Add the almonds and paprika; cook, stirring often, for 5 minutes, or until the almonds are golden. Immediately remove to a bowl to stop the cooking (the almonds may burn otherwise).

In a bowl, combine the lemon juice, the remaining ¼ cup of olive oil, the remaining ¼ teaspoon of salt, the pepper, the toasted almonds, and the dill. Pour over the zucchini. Toss to distribute the dressing. Taste for salt and adjust if needed. Let rest for up to 30 minutes and serve at room temperature.

juicing citrus No need for fancy reamers and citrus presses. All you need to get the most juice out of your lemons, limes, oranges, and grapefruit is to roll the fruit back and forth along the work surface as you apply pressure, then cut the fruit in half and squeeze each half forcefully with one hand as you place your other hand beneath to catch any seeds or membranes. Some cooks also prick citrus fruit with a fork after rolling it, before squeezing.

smoky pepper strips in lemony caper marinade

peperoni con salsina di capperi e limone /// SERVES 4

1 red bell pepper, halved,
  seeded, and cut into eighths
1 yellow bell pepper, halved,
  seeded, and cut into eighths
1 orange bell pepper, halved,
  seeded, and cut into eighths
¼ cup plus 1 tablespoon extra-
  virgin olive oil
Grated zest of 1 large or 2 small
  lemons
2 garlic cloves, halved
3 tablespoons salted capers,
  rinsed and chopped
¼ teaspoon salt
¼ teaspoon freshly ground black
  pepper
1 tablespoon minced oregano

cook's note Select an assortment of sweet bell peppers for this delicious side dish: orange, red, and yellow look glorious combined. But avoid using green bell peppers, which are not sweet enough to complement the lemon–caper dressing.

I am reminded of Sicily every time I make this lovely side dish. The vibrant flavor of lemon zest, the savory bite of capers, and the gentle aroma of oregano suffuse the peppers with a truly magical taste. The same marinade can be used with grilled fish; it would do especially well with hake or monkfish.

Heat a grill to a medium flame.

Toss the red, yellow, and orange peppers with 1 tablespoon of the olive oil.

Place the peppers on the grill and cook, stirring from time to time, for about 10 minutes, or until they are lightly charred and softened. Place the grilled peppers on a large serving platter while you make the marinade.

In a medium bowl, whisk together the remaining ¼ cup of olive oil, the lemon zest, garlic, capers, salt, pepper, and oregano.

Pour the lemon–caper marinade over the grilled peppers and allow to marinate for 15 minutes at room temperature or up to 2 days in the refrigerator. Serve at room temperature.

making garlic easier to digest
Whether you eat it raw or cooked, garlic can be hard to digest, so here's a trick to make it more digestible. Before you crush, chop, or mince garlic, remove any bruised or browned spots, including the little flat end, which often turns dark and hard. Slit the clove in half vertically and discard the inner germ, which changes from white to green to brown as the garlic ages. The darker the germ, the more bitter and difficult to digest it will be.

fennel wedges in tarragon-laced balsamic vinaigrette

finocchi con vinaigrette all'aceto balsamico e dragoncello /// SERVES 4

2 fennel bulbs, trimmed, quartered, and cut into 1/2-inch-thick wedges

1 tablespoon plus 1 teaspoon salt

1/3 cup plus 2 tablespoons extra-virgin olive oil

1/4 teaspoon freshly ground black pepper

2 shallots, very thinly sliced

1/4 cup minced tarragon or 1 tablespoon dried tarragon

2 tablespoons authentic balsamic vinegar (see Note)

cook's note Genuine balsamic vinegar (not the stuff sold for five dollars a gallon in supermarkets) is produced only in and around the city of Modena in Emilia-Romagna from the fermented must of Trebbiano and other indigenous grapes. To be sure you are buying the real thing rather than an imitation, look for the words "Consorzio Produttori Aceto Balsamico Tradizionale di Modena" on the bottle.

I have always adored fennel: I love it raw, sautéed, fried, grilled, braised . . . there isn't a fennel dish I've tried that I haven't enjoyed. The subtle licorice flavor of fennel pairs especially well with fresh tarragon. Look for pale green fennel bulbs with their fronds and stalks still attached, and trim off the tough outer layer and the dark base before quartering and cutting the bulb into wedges. Female fennel, which are rounder and more "hippy" in appearance than male, are sweeter and milder. Blanching the fennel before grilling it tames its potentially fibrous texture and makes it silky soft.

Bring 2 quarts of water to a boil. Drop in the fennel wedges and 1 tablespoon of the salt and cook for 10 minutes. Drain and rinse under cool water to stop the cooking.

Heat a grill to a high flame.

Toss the fennel wedges with 2 tablespoons of the olive oil, 1/2 teaspoon of the salt, and 1/8 teaspoon of the pepper. Grill the fennel wedges, turning once, until lightly softened and tinged with brown on both sides, about 4 minutes per side. Arrange the grilled fennel on a platter and cool to room temperature.

Meanwhile, place the shallots, tarragon, balsamic vinegar, and the remaining 1/3 cup of olive oil, 1/2 teaspoon of salt, and 1/8 teaspoon of pepper in a jar. Close with a tight-fitting lid and shake vigorously (the mixture will not emulsify or become creamy; the dressing can be made up to 24 hours in advance and kept refrigerated).

Pour the dressing over the grilled fennel wedges. Taste for salt, adjust if needed, and serve within 1 hour.

warm vinaigrettes and bitter lettuces: a marriage made in heaven There are some flavor combinations that cannot be improved upon: fresh bread with bittersweet chocolate, tomatoes with olive oil, garlic with parsley . . . and warm vinaigrettes with bitter lettuces definitely fall into this category. There is something about the flavor of reduced vinegar paired with bitter greens, something about the warm dressing coating the leaves of lettuce, that is sheer magic. While more buttery, delicate lettuces like Boston or oak leaf can certainly be tossed with a warm dressing, the best candidates for this treatment are sturdy, bitter greens like frisée, radicchio, and endive. When a warm vinaigrette is poured over raw greens, the leaves wilt instantly and absorb the dressing. And when a warm vinaigrette is poured over grilled greens, like wedges of radicchio, the dressing pools deliciously between the layers of leaves, and the greens' bitterness is tamed by the dressing's acidity.

radicchio in warm vinegar dressing

radicchio con vinaigrette tiepida /// SERVES 2 TO 4

2 heads of radicchio di Treviso
(6 ounces each), halved
lengthwise

1 tablespoon plus ½ teaspoon
salt

¼ cup extra-virgin olive oil

¼ teaspoon freshly ground black
pepper

¼ pound pancetta, diced

2 large or 3 medium shallots,
thinly sliced

¼ cup red-wine vinegar

cook's note Endive can be cooked
the exact same way as radicchio di
Treviso. Try grilling a combination of
endive and radicchio for a striking
presentation.

Treviso is one of the Veneto's most beautiful cities, dotted with canals and windmills and home to a bustling outdoor market. One of the stars at the greengrocers' stands in Treviso is a prized variety of elongated radicchio. Radicchio di Treviso resembles a Belgian endive but is delicately crinkly rather than flat, with a deep burgundy color and stark white ribs. Like its cousin, the round radicchio from Chioggia (see photograph, opposite) that is most commonly found in North America, radicchio di Treviso is markedly bitter; but its bitterness can be tamed by blanching, a process that also makes it silky tender.

Bring 2 quarts of water to a boil. Drop in the radicchio and 1 tablespoon of the salt and cook for 2 minutes, or just until the radicchio wilts. Drain and rinse under cool water to stop the cooking. Very gently squeeze out the excess water, trying to keep the radicchio halves intact.

Toss the radicchio with 1 tablespoon of the olive oil, ¼ teaspoon of the salt, and ⅛ teaspoon of the pepper.

Heat a grill to a high flame.

Grill the radicchio until it is lightly softened and tinged with brown on both sides, turning once, about 3 minutes per side. Transfer to a platter.

Heat a 12-inch sauté pan over a medium flame. Add the pancetta and shallots and cook until the pancetta browns lightly and the shallots wilt, about 10 minutes. Raise the heat to high and stand back from the pan. Pour in the vinegar and cook until it reduces to a glaze, about 1 minute. Add the remaining 3 tablespoons of olive oil, ¼ teaspoon of salt, and ⅛ teaspoon of pepper, and swirl gently to combine. Pour the warm vinaigrette over the radicchio and serve immediately.

sicilian pepper bundles

involtini di peperoni delle isole eolie /// SERVES 4

4 red bell peppers

4 yellow bell peppers

1 cup fresh bread crumbs

¼ cup salted capers, rinsed
and chopped

1 small garlic clove, very finely
minced

2 tablespoons minced oregano

12 basil leaves, minced

¼ cup freshly grated pecorino
romano

¼ cup extra-virgin olive oil

¼ teaspoon salt

¼ teaspoon freshly ground black
pepper

cook's note I like a combination of red and yellow bell peppers for this dish, because they look so pretty alternating on the skewers. If you wish, you can top slices of grilled eggplant with the bread-crumb stuffing, roll them into bundles, and thread them onto skewers, alternating them with the pepper bundles.

I enjoyed this festive dish bursting with the colors and flavors of summer in Sicily many years ago. It is a favorite preparation on the Aeolian Islands, the small volcanic islands (Lipari, Panarea, Alicudi, Filicudi, Vulcano, Salina, and Stromboli) scattered off the northeastern coast of Sicily. The Greeks colonized these islands around 580 B.C. and named them after the mythical figure Aeolus, a god-king who kept the winds bottled in a cave; the nickname of these still-wild, scarcely populated islands is "Sicily's Home of the Winds," because they are racked by fierce gusts. Lipari is the main island and the one with the most tourist amenities; some of the smaller islands, particularly Panarea, have recently become favorites among the jet set.

Heat a grill to a high flame.

If using wooden skewers, soak 16 skewers in water to cover for 30 minutes; drain.

Place the whole peppers on the grill. Grill until the skin is blackened all over and the flesh is soft, 15 to 30 minutes, turning every few minutes with tongs to cook evenly. The peppers should be nearly collapsing when done.

Remove to a bowl and cover tightly with aluminum foil. Set aside for 30 minutes; the steam created in the covered bowl will help loosen the skin from the flesh of the peppers. Uncover the bowl and slip the skin off the peppers with your fingers. Even if you are tempted to run the peppers under cool water to remove bits of clinging skin, don't do it: You would be rinsing away the delicious smoky flavor. If needed, use a clean towel to wipe away clinging bits of skin from the peppers.

Cut the peppers in half, scoop out the seeds, stem, and any membrane, and cut each half into 2 long, wide strips. You will have 32 pepper strips in all.

In a bowl, combine the bread crumbs, capers, garlic, oregano, basil, pecorino, olive oil, salt, and pepper.

Lay the roasted pepper strips on a work surface, with the side that was attached to the skin facing down. Sprinkle the caper–bread crumb mixture evenly over the pepper strips. Roll into tight bundles.

Thread the pepper bundles onto the skewers, alternating red and yellow; thread the bundles onto two skewers, not just one, to prevent them from spinning when you try to turn them on the grill. You will have 8 double skewers, each holding 4 bundles.

Return to the hot grill and cook until heated through, about 2 minutes per side, turning once. Be careful when you turn the skewers, as the bread-crumb stuffing may leak out.

Serve the skewers hot, warm, or at room temperature.

my mother's grilled peppers **In the summer, my mother grills huge quantities of peppers and packs them in canning jars with a few garlic cloves and olive oil to cover, then freezes the jars for the winter. If you're feeling industrious or you have way too many peppers on your hands, you can do the same. The peppers will keep in the freezer for up to 4 months. Grill the peppers whole until they become very soft (see page 120), then peel, seed, and cut them into strips. Toss the grilled pepper strips with a quintessentially Italian marinade: slivers of raw garlic, basil leaves, olive oil, and salt. You can add vinegar and pepper, if you like, for a more bracing flavor.**

sardinian eggplant purée with white wine and garlic

puré di melanzane con vino bianco ed aglio alla sarda /// SERVES 4

2 medium eggplants (1 pound
    each)
2 garlic cloves, peeled
3/4 teaspoon salt
2 tablespoons dry white wine
1/4 cup extra-virgin olive oil
1/4 teaspoon freshly ground black
    pepper

cook's note I can't stress how important it is to cook the eggplants until they become *absolutely* tender. Don't pull them off the grill until they have become black all over and are so soft that they start to ooze juice on the grill, their flesh literally falling apart. That is when the smokiness of the grill will have penetrated the eggplants' skin and the flavor will be superb. Eggplants that are cooked any less will be tough and stringy and won't make a nice purée.

My friends Efisio and Francesco Farris own Pomodoro and Arcodoro, two fabulous Sardinian restaurants in Houston and Dallas. Every time I am in either city we find a way to get together. This recipe is an adaptation of their addictive smoked eggplant purée flavored with white wine, olive oil, and garlic. Serve it as they would, with a crisp Sardinian flatbread called pane carasau (see Mail-Order Sources, page 183), or with grilled ciabatta or country bread as a starter. You can also offer the eggplant purée in non-Sardinian fashion as a topping for grilled fish or poultry, or as a pasta sauce.

Heat a grill to a medium-high flame.

Prick the eggplants with a fork to prevent bursting. Grill, turning every few minutes, until the skin is blistered and blackened all over and the flesh is extremely soft when pierced with a fork, 35 to 45 minutes. To achieve the desired creaminess, cook the eggplants until they nearly collapse and become very soft; they will look scary, but the flavor will be perfect (see Note).

Using two spatulas, remove the eggplants to a platter. Slit them in half lengthwise and, using two spoons, pick out as many of the seeds as possible; the seeds are bitter. (It is better to discard more rather than less—I usually remove about one-fifth of the eggplant by picking out the seeds.)

Scoop out the flesh from the eggplant skin and place in a sieve set over a bowl; drain at room temperature for 2 hours. Discard the bitter, dark liquid in the bowl.

Transfer the drained eggplant flesh to a clean bowl. Using a fork, beat the eggplant until it breaks down into a creamy purée; some chunks will still be visible, and that's fine. Don't use a food processor to purée the eggplant, or it will be watery and uninteresting in texture.

In a mortar with a pestle, crush the garlic with the salt into a creamy paste. Add the garlic paste to the eggplant purée. Stir in the wine, olive oil, and pepper, and taste for seasoning; adjust if needed. Serve at room temperature, with grilled bread.

eggplant varieties There are dozens of varieties of eggplant cultivated around the world. The most common in North America is a dark purple-skinned, oval eggplant that weighs around $1/2$ pound when small and over 1 pound when large; these have a fair number of seeds and a compact, somewhat bitter flesh. Japanese and Chinese eggplants are elongated in shape, with lighter skin; creamier, pale flesh; and fewer seeds. White eggplants can be round or egg-shaped (it is the latter that led to eggplant's curious name); they are very firm, with thicker skin than purple varieties and a more pronounced bitterness. Striated varieties also exist in various shapes and sizes. And then there are the squat mauve-skinned round eggplants known as Prosperosa, reminiscent of those grown in Italy; these are my favorites, as their flavor is more buttery and their skin very delicate, but they can be difficult to find.

eggplant coins with chunky walnut–chive salsa

melanzane con vinaigrette di noci ed erba cipollina /// SERVES 12

1 medium eggplant (about
    1 pound), sliced into ¼-inch-
    thick coins
1 tablespoon plus ½ teaspoon-
    salt
¼ cup plus ⅓ cup extra-virgin
    olive oil
2 tablespoons fresh lemon juice
½ cup snipped chives
2 tablespoons tarragon leaves
½ cup shelled walnut halves,
    chopped
¼ teaspoon freshly ground
    black pepper

cook's note The same sauce can be paired with blanched and grilled fennel wedges (see page 117) or blanched and grilled leeks (see page 129) instead of eggplant.

This is a surprising dish, and one that might just turn the most devout eggplant hater into an eggplant lover. The walnut salsa is loosely based on a pasta sauce I've experienced (and loved!) in Liguria, but I add lemon juice and herbs to perk it up; after all, eggplant needs vibrant, bold partners to shine. Be sure to refrigerate walnuts and other nuts, rather than keep them at room temperature in the pantry, where they risk becoming rancid. The one thing to remember about eggplant—be it fried, grilled, baked, or sautéed—is that if it is anything less than fully cooked, it will be unpleasantly bitter and leathery; so please cook it all the way through before pulling it off the grill.

Sprinkle the eggplant with 1 tablespoon of the salt. Place it in a colander set over a bowl and let it purge its bitter liquid for 30 minutes. Rinse and blot dry.

Brush the eggplant slices on both sides with ¼ cup of the olive oil. Heat a grill to a medium-high flame.

Grill the eggplant until it is browned on the outside and soft on the inside, about 5 minutes per side, turning once. Don't undercook the eggplant or it will be unpleasantly bitter; a fully cooked eggplant should be creamy and white inside, with no trace of green and no chewiness. If the eggplant starts to burn before it has a chance to cook through, move it to a cooler part of the grill. Cool to room temperature.

Meanwhile, purée the lemon juice, chives, tarragon, walnuts, the remaining ½ teaspoon of salt, and the pepper in a blender or food processor until a coarse paste forms. With the motor running, pour in the remaining ⅓ cup of olive oil; a chunky dressing will form. (This can be done up to 12 hours ahead; whisk with a fork before serving if the dressing separates and the oil floats to the top.)

Spoon the walnut dressing over the grilled eggplant coins and serve within 5 minutes.

caramelized tomatoes with oregano and garlic

pomodori alla pizzaiola /// SERVES 4

8 ripe plum tomatoes, halved
   lengthwise

3 tablespoons extra-virgin
   olive oil

¾ teaspoon salt

¼ teaspoon freshly ground
   black pepper

1 tablespoon minced oregano

8 garlic cloves, halved

cook's note You can use plum tomatoes, beefsteak tomatoes, or any variety you fancy—as long as they are really ripe and flavorful. And if fresh oregano is unavailable, reach for fresh marjoram or thyme instead.

Delicious, easy to make, and so versatile: These tomatoes taste great alone, alongside meat or fish, crushed on top of grilled bread, or chopped and tossed with boiled pasta. They remind me of the beef alla pizzaiola that my mother used to make when I was little: thin slices of beef cooked with tomatoes, oregano, and olive oil, then topped with a slice of mozzarella at the last moment.

Heat a grill to a medium-high flame.

In a bowl, toss the tomatoes with 1 tablespoon of the olive oil, the salt, the pepper, and the oregano.

Insert a garlic half into each tomato half, embedding it securely inside the tomato flesh (or it will burn if it comes in contact with the grill). Place the tomatoes, cut side down, on the grill. Grill until the tomatoes are just beginning to soften and caramelize, about 10 minutes. Turn and cook until the other side is also starting to soften and to become lightly charred, 5 to 10 more minutes. Do not overcook, or the tomatoes will fall apart.

Transfer to a serving platter, cut side up. Drizzle with the remaining 2 tablespoons of olive oil, adjust the seasoning if needed, and serve hot, warm, or at room temperature.

storing tomatoes **Don't store tomatoes in the refrigerator. Their sugars will become dormant in the cold, making them less sweet and more mealy. Store tomatoes at room temperature and eat them within a few days, before they soften too much. But don't despair if your tomatoes get a little mushy before you've had a chance to eat them: Soft tomatoes are delicious cooked in sauces, sautés, soups, and on the grill.**

seared asparagus with lemon zest and chives

asparagi con buccia di limone ed erba cipollina /// SERVES 4

1 bunch of asparagus (¾ pound),
 woody ends trimmed

3 tablespoons extra-virgin
 olive oil

8 thick, long-stemmed rosemary
 sprigs

2 strips of lemon zest, julienned

2 garlic cloves, slivered

¼ cup snipped chives

½ teaspoon salt

¼ teaspoon freshly ground black
 pepper

cook's note For a more intense rose-mary aroma, scatter the rosemary sprigs directly on the coals rather than using them as a base for the aspara-gus on the grill grate; or if your grill has a smoker box, place the rosemary sprigs in an aluminum-foil pouch in the smoker box.

Grilled asparagus are delightfully crunchy and intense. I love them even more when they are slow-grilled atop aromatic rosemary or thyme sprigs. The herbs suffuse the asparagus with an intoxicating aroma. Remember, however, to line the grill grate with a sheet of aluminum foil to prevent the sprigs from burning. If you are cooking thick asparagus, cook them over a moderate flame or the outsides may burn before the insides are tender.

Heat a grill to a medium-high flame.

Toss the asparagus with 1 tablespoon of the olive oil. Place a sheet of aluminum foil on the grill grate. Arrange the rosemary sprigs on the aluminum foil and then place the asparagus perpen-dicularly over the rosemary sprigs.

Grill until the asparagus softens and becomes lightly browned all over, turning every minute or so to ensure even cooking; it will take 10 to 15 minutes depending on the thickness. The asparagus will still be crisp-tender. (If you wish, move the asparagus directly over the flames and away from the rosemary and aluminum foil for a minute or two to create strong grill marks.)

Remove the asparagus to a platter. Discard the grilled rosemary sprigs. Add the lemon zest, garlic, chives, salt, pepper, and the remaining 2 tablespoons of olive oil. Toss to coat well and serve hot, warm, or at room temperature.

julienning citrus zest To julienne lemon zest (or the zest of any citrus) using a knife:

1. Peel the zest from the lemon using a vegetable peeler, obtaining long, thin strips of zest much like carrot shavings, being sure to avoid the bitter white pith beneath the color-ful zest.

2. Stack 2 to 3 strips of the zest on a cutting board.

3. With a sharp chef's knife, cut the strips into fine hair-like threads; this is the julienne.

 You can also buy a handy citrus zester, which looks similar to a bottle opener, and shave off the zest in a fine julienne.

scallions with spicy almond pesto

scalogni con pesto piccante alle mandorle /// SERVES 6

½ cup plus 2 tablespoons extra-
virgin olive oil

⅔ cup blanched almonds

1 small garlic clove, peeled

1 medium ripe tomato, peeled,
seeded, and diced (see
page 149)

¼ teaspoon hot paprika

⅛ teaspoon cayenne pepper

½ teaspoon salt

½ cup Italian parsley leaves

2 tablespoons red-wine vinegar

24 scallions (1 pound before
trimming), trimmed and
washed (see Note)

cook's note The white part of scallions is much sweeter than the green tops. When using scallions raw, I generally don't use any of the pungent green part. When scallions are grilled, the potency of the green part is tamed, so I include the green parts too. To prepare the scallions for grilling, trim the beards if they are really long, but leave them attached as they will hold the layers together. Cut off about ½ inch of the dark green portion. Rinse the scallions thoroughly, rubbing well with your fingers to dislodge any sand caught between the layers.

The pesto that is served with these scallions is a variant on one made in Trapani, Sicily, as a sauce for pasta. I add vinegar for a bright note, and a hint of paprika and cayenne for a spicy kick.

Heat an 8-inch skillet over a medium flame. Add 1 tablespoon of the olive oil and the almonds, and toast the almonds until they take on a nutty scent and a golden color, stirring constantly to avoid burning, about 5 minutes. Immediately remove to a bowl, cool, and then transfer to a blender.

Add the garlic to the almonds in the blender and pulse until a paste forms. Add the tomato, paprika, cayenne, salt, parsley, and vinegar, and pulse until combined. With the motor running, dribble in ½ cup of the olive oil in a thin, steady stream; the mixture will emulsify. Transfer to a bowl; set aside at room temperature until needed (the pesto can be made up to 12 hours ahead). If the pesto separates, stir it vigorously.

Heat a grill to a high flame.

Toss the scallions with the remaining tablespoon of olive oil and grill until lightly blackened all over and soft, about 5 minutes, turning often to cook evenly. Be careful not to burn the delicate green parts.

Serve the scallions hot, passing the pesto around the table. I like to dip the white part of the scallions into the pesto and, holding the scallion from the green part, nibble away.

storing nuts Because of their high fat content, nuts are especially susceptible to rancidity. To keep nuts fresh, store them in the refrigerator (up to 2 months) or in the freezer (up to 6 months), then return to room temperature before eating or incorporating them in your recipe. The cold will not affect the nuts' flavor or texture, but it will slow down their deterioration.

leeks in pink peppercorn vinaigrette

porri con vinaigrette al pepe rosa /// SERVES 4

6 small leeks (2 pounds untrimmed weight), white parts only, halved lengthwise

1 tablespoon plus ½ teaspoon salt

6 tablespoons extra-virgin olive oil

1 teaspoon Dijon mustard

1 tablespoon red-wine vinegar

2 tablespoons minced tarragon leaves or ½ tablespoon dried tarragon

1 teaspoon snipped chives

2 shallots, minced

1 garlic clove, minced

¼ teaspoon crushed black-peppercorns

½ teaspoon crushed pink peppercorns

cook's note To crush the pink and black peppercorns, use a mortar and pestle, or wrap them in a towel and crush with the bottom of a heavy pan.

My mother-in-law, Claude-Marie, is famous for her steamed leeks in a creamy mustard and pink peppercorn dressing. Those leeks were the highlight of many family dinners, and now that I live far from my in-laws, I often crave Claude-Marie's dish. Leeks belong to the onion family, and when they are grilled after blanching, their delicate onion flavor is intensified. Select thin young leeks with full beards and their green tops still attached, then trim them so only the tender white part gets cooked; the trimmings can be used in stocks.

Rinse the leeks thoroughly under cool water, fanning out the layers and running your fingers between them to dislodge any grit.

Bring 2 quarts of water to a boil. Add the leeks and 1 tablespoon of the salt and cook for 5 minutes, or until almost tender when pierced with a knife. Drain, rinse under cool water to stop the cooking, and blot dry very gently.

Heat a grill to a high flame.

Gently toss the blanched leeks with 1 tablespoon of the olive oil and ¼ teaspoon of the salt. Grill until lightly browned and tender, about 3 minutes per side, turning once. Remove to a platter.

In a medium bowl, combine the mustard, vinegar, and the remaining ¼ teaspoon of salt. Beating with a wire whisk all the while, pour in the remaining 5 tablespoons of olive oil in a thin steady stream, until well blended and emulsified. Whisk in the tarragon, chives, shallots, garlic, black peppercorns, and pink peppercorns. Pour the dressing over the leeks. Let rest for 30 minutes or up to 4 hours, and serve at room temperature.

baby artichokes with fresh mint

carciofi alla menta /// SERVES 4

16 baby artichokes, trimmed (see sidebar)

1 lemon, halved

¼ cup extra-virgin olive oil

½ teaspoon salt

¼ teaspoon freshly ground black pepper

1 garlic clove, minced

2 tablespoons minced mint

cook's note Mint and artichokes go beautifully together: The mint's vibrant, peppery flavor cuts through the artichoke's tannins. The pairing is typical of southern Italy, where mint and artichokes thrive.

trimming artichokes To trim an artichoke, begin by removing the tough outer leaves. Cut away the cone of hard leaves at the top. Remove the hairy inner choke with a melon baller or small spoon; any fuzz will be very hard to digest, so be sure to scoop it all out. Immediately rub with a cut lemon to prevent the artichoke from turning black, and drop into a bowl of cool water with 2 tablespoons of lemon juice. Cook the artichokes as soon as possible, as they oxidize quickly upon contact with the air.

Artichokes are members of the thistle family, descendants of the wild cardoons enjoyed in ancient Rome and across the Mediterranean basin for thousands of years. Although some culinary historians believe artichokes evolved in North Africa, others trace their birth to Sicily. Either way, artichokes are one of Italy's most emblematic vegetables: Italy is the world's largest artichoke producer, with Liguria, Tuscany, Latium, Apulia, Sicily, and Sardinia leading the way. Baby artichokes are prized above all. They are eaten raw, their delicate leaves dipped whole in fruity olive oil or slivered into paper-thin ribbons to be doused with lemon juice and olive oil as a delectable starter. When selecting artichokes for the grill, opt for baby artichokes, which cook up tender and delicious within minutes. If you can't find baby artichokes, large globe artichokes will do; halve them, blanch them for 3 minutes in boiling water, then proceed with the recipe below.

Rub the artichokes all over, especially on the cut surfaces, with a lemon half. Toss with 1 tablespoon of the olive oil and ¼ teaspoon of the salt.

In a serving bowl, combine the remaining 3 tablespoons of olive oil, the remaining ¼ teaspoon of salt, the pepper, garlic, and mint. Squeeze the remaining lemon half into the mint mixture in the bowl.

Heat a grill to a high flame.

Place the artichokes on the grill. Grill for 5 to 10 minutes, or until browned lightly and just soft, turning as needed to cook evenly. Toss while still hot with the mint mixture and serve hot, warm, or at room temperature.

vegetable skewers in three-herb pesto over baby greens

spiedini di verdure estive /// SERVES 4

FOR THE SKEWERS

6 shiitake or button mushrooms, stemmed and halved

1 small zucchini, quartered lengthwise and cut into 12 cubes

1 medium purple onion, quartered and cut into 12 cubes

12 cherry tomatoes

FOR THE HERB PESTO

1/2 cup packed basil leaves

1/2 cup packed tarragon leaves

1/2 cup snipped chives

2 small garlic cloves, peeled

1 teaspoon salt

1/2 teaspoon freshly ground black pepper

1/2 teaspoon fennel seeds, coarsely crushed in a mortar

1/8 teaspoon dried red pepper flakes (optional)

2/3 cup extra-virgin olive oil

TO SERVE

3 cups mesclun (mixed baby greens), washed and dried (see Note)

1 lemon, cut into wedges

Grilled vegetables with herb-infused olive oil are a classic offering on Italian tables, especially in the summertime, when basil and other fragrant herbs are at their aromatic peak.

Make the skewers: If using wooden skewers, soak 4 wooden skewers in water to cover for 30 minutes; drain.

Thread the mushrooms, zucchini, onion, and tomatoes onto the skewers, alternating 3 pieces of each on each skewer.

Heat a grill to a high flame.

Make the pesto: Combine all the ingredients except the olive oil in a blender. With the motor running, add the olive oil in a thin stream until emulsified; taste for salt, adjust if needed, and set aside.

Brush the skewered vegetables with 2 tablespoons of the pesto. Grill, turning as needed to cook evenly, until the vegetables are lightly charred on the outside and tender, 5 to 10 minutes total.

To serve: Line a platter with the mesclun. Place the skewers over the mesclun. Pour on some of the remaining herb pesto, garnish with the lemon wedges, and serve hot, warm, or at room temperature, passing additional herb pesto around the table.

cook's note If you're tired of throwing out lettuce because it gets limp, wash it, keeping the leaves whole, and dry thoroughly. Place in a bowl and cover with a double thickness of paper towels moistened with water. The lettuce will remain crisp for 2 days in the refrigerator.

no more spinning skewers
When threading small items on skewers, I like to use 2 skewers rather than a single one. Not only is the food held more securely, it also won't spin around annoyingly when you turn the skewers on the grill. To make threading food on a double skewer easier, line up 2 skewers parallel to each other on a work surface and thread the food on the 2 skewers at the same time.

herb-basted portobello mushroom caps

funghi in graticola /// SERVES 2 TO 4

¼ cup extra-virgin olive oil

¾ teaspoon salt

¼ teaspoon freshly ground
black pepper

1 garlic clove, minced

1 tablespoon minced Italian
parsley

4 large, perfect portobello
mushroom caps (about
2 ounces each), cleaned

cook's note Portobellos are over-
grown cremini mushrooms; they have
a deep, earthy flavor and a rich, meaty
texture.

The trio of olive oil, garlic, and parsley forms the basis of so many dishes in
Italian cuisine. When mushrooms are sautéed with these ingredients, they are
referred to as trifolati. If you can find fresh porcini mushrooms, their brown
caps meaty and dark, by all means grill them as below.

Heat a grill to a high flame.

In a small bowl, combine 2 tablespoons of the olive oil, the salt,
pepper, garlic, and parsley. Add the mushroom caps and toss very
gently to coat well on all sides.

Place the mushroom caps, rounded side down, on the grill for
4 minutes, or until nicely browned and starting to soften. Turn and
grill until browned on the other side and soft, about 4 more minutes.

Remove to a platter and drizzle with the remaining 2 tablespoons
of olive oil. Serve hot, warm, or at room temperature, adjusting the
salt if needed.

porcini, italy's favorite
mushrooms **Porcini, known as
cèpes in French, are among the most
prized mushrooms anywhere in the
world. Their rich, meaty flavor and
succulent texture make them favorites for grilling, stewing, and sautéing,
and their intense aroma when dried is
intoxicating in risottos, soups, and
stews. (The most curious use I ever
encountered for porcini was in Calabria, where a local distiller makes
porcini-flavored grappa!) All porcini
belong to the *Boletus* family, which
encompasses various species; the
most common is *Boletus edulis,* a variety that grows spontaneously across
Italy from north to south. Italians reg-
ularly head into the countryside to
forage for mushrooms, especially
porcini, but the activity is strictly reg-
ulated by the Italian government,
which imposes stiff penalties for picking porcini in a way that could prove
harmful to their reproduction or their
natural environment. Mushrooms too
small to have reproduced (with caps
less than 3 centimeters, or just over
an inch, in diameter) are off limits. All
mushrooms must be picked by hand,
without aid of knives or rakes, which
could damage the soil. Mushroom for-
aging is only permitted on certain
days of the week, and only during
daylight hours. And most of all, for-
agers must have a valid forager's ID
card, purchased at national parks
societies, county offices, and so on
across Italy. The goal is to preserve
wild *Boletus* and other mushrooms
for future generations. To order fresh,
frozen, or dried porcini, check the
Mail-Order Sources (page 183).**

paying homage to leftover bread In the Mediterranean kitchen, bread is sacred. My mother, whom I've seen pour out the contents of a half-finished Champagne bottle after a dinner party, bristles at the thought of throwing away bread: Anything more substantial than a crumb gets recycled. And so all across Italy, there are dozens of soups, salads, sauces, stuffings, and even desserts that pay homage to leftover bread. When I was little, my grandmother made a sauce with crustless leftover bread, olive oil, lemon juice, garlic, and egg whites—it was sort of like mayonnaise, but less rich, and absolutely pungent with raw garlic. We ate the sauce slathered on bread, a fitting tribute to a sacred food.

fire-kissed tuscan bread and tomato salad

panzanella alla griglia /// SERVES 8

60 cherry tomatoes (1½ pounds)

2 medium purple onions, peel on, scored lengthwise to prevent splitting

½ pound crustless day-old bread, cut into ½-inch-thick slices

1 English cucumber, peel on, cut into ¼-inch dice

¼ cup capers in brine, drained

¼ cup red-wine vinegar

¾ cup extra-virgin olive oil

1 teaspoon salt

¼ teaspoon freshly ground black pepper

20 basil leaves, torn

cook's note Tuscan cooks—and cooks in nearby Umbria and the Marches—prefer saltless bread. If you can't find saltless bread at your local bakery, a country bread with a thick, chewy crust and a dense crumb will be fine as long as it isn't flavored with anything: no garlic or herbs, no olives, no sun-dried tomatoes—just flour, yeast, salt, and water. The bland, wheaty flavor of the bread will serve as the perfect canvas for this delectable salad.

Panzanella is one of Tuscany's greatest exports; over the past decade it has appeared on restaurant menus and on kitchen tables across North America. At its simplest, panzanella is a salad of day-old bread, fresh basil, sweet tomatoes, and onions splashed with vinegar and fruity olive oil. This salad is a takeoff on classic panzanella. Grilling the tomatoes, onions, and bread results in a more intensely savory flavor; I add diced cucumbers and capers, which are sometimes included in traditional panzanella, for a vibrant note.

If using wooden skewers, soak 10 skewers in water to cover for 30 minutes; drain.

Heat a grill to a high flame.

Thread the cherry tomatoes onto the skewers. Grill the skewered cherry tomatoes until they soften and the skins char lightly, 5 to 10 minutes, turning as needed to cook evenly. Don't cook the cherry tomatoes too long or they will burst on the grill. Remove from the skewers to a serving bowl and cool to room temperature.

Grill the onions until the skins become black and the flesh softens, about 25 minutes. Slip off the skins and charred outer layer. Chop coarsely and add to the cherry tomatoes.

Grill the bread until it is lightly browned on both sides, about 2 minutes per side, turning once. Coarsely crumble into the bowl with the cherry tomatoes and onions.

Add the cucumber, capers, vinegar, olive oil, salt, and pepper, and mash lightly with your hands to encourage the tomatoes and bread to break down slightly; the longer you mash the ingredients, the more of a pap-like consistency you will obtain. Taste for salt and adjust if needed. Let rest for 30 minutes (or up to 2 hours) at room temperature.

Fold in the basil and serve.

baby yukon gold potatoes with sage and white wine

patatine novelle con salvia e vino bianco /// SERVES 6

1 cup dry white wine

1 bay leaf

1 tablespoon plus ½ teaspoon salt

1 quart water

1 pound baby Yukon Gold potatoes, peel on, halved if small or quartered if large

¼ teaspoon freshly ground black pepper

2 tablespoons extra-virgin olive oil

2 tablespoons minced sage

4 garlic cloves, chopped coarsely

cook's note I prefer baby Yukon Gold potatoes for roasting and grilling. Neither too starchy nor too waxy, they have compact, creamy flesh with a lovely golden color. If baby Yukon Golds aren't available, try fingerlings instead.

This all-purpose side dish pairs nicely with poultry and lamb: potatoes are boiled until tender in water and white wine perfumed with a bay leaf, then tossed with sage and garlic and grilled to a gorgeous golden brown. You can treat parsnips or butternut squash much the same way, or prepare a combination of the three.

Select 4 thick, sturdy skewers strong enough to hold up under the weight of the potatoes. If using wooden skewers, soak in water to cover for 30 minutes; drain.

Heat a grill to a high flame.

Meanwhile, combine the white wine, bay leaf, 1 tablespoon of the salt, and the water in a 3-quart pot. Add the potatoes and bring to a gentle boil over medium heat. Cook, uncovered, for 10 to 15 minutes, or until the potatoes are just tender when pierced with a knife.

Drain the potatoes. Toss with the remaining ½ teaspoon of salt, the pepper, olive oil, sage, and garlic.

Thread the potatoes onto the skewers. Place the skewers on the grill and cook 5 to 10 minutes, turning as needed to brown evenly. Serve hot.

summer vegetable millefoglie in basil oil [PHOTOGRAPH ON PAGE 139]

millefoglie di verdure estive con basilico /// SERVES 4

6 red bell peppers

1 teaspoon salt

¼ teaspoon freshly ground black
  pepper

6 tablespoons extra-virgin olive
  oil, plus extra for greasing the
  ramekins

1 small zucchini, cut lengthwise
  into ¼-inch-thick ribbons

¾ cup fresh whole-milk ricotta

3 tablespoons freshly grated
  pecorino romano

¼ cup snipped chives

6 basil leaves, finely minced

½ small garlic clove, peeled

cook's note You will need small, indi-
vidual ramekins or soufflé molds to
layer the ingredients. You can also
make one large millefoglie, but it will
be hard to portion and would lose its
lovely structure once cut.

Elegant, delicious, and original, this millefoglie (literally, "thousand leaves")
doesn't call for any pastry, making it much lighter than classic millefoglie.
Grilled bell pepper strips are layered with a creamy ricotta stuffing and
enclosed in thin ribbons of grilled zucchini, a perfect dish for a light summer
lunch. You can use marjoram or oregano instead of chives in the ricotta stuffing, but avoid strong herbs like rosemary or sage, which would overwhelm the
delicate taste of the vegetables.

Heat a grill to a high flame.

Grill the peppers until the skin is blackened all over and the flesh
is soft, 15 to 30 minutes, turning every few minutes with tongs to
cook evenly. The peppers should be nearly collapsing when done.

Remove to a bowl and cover tightly with aluminum foil. Set aside
for 30 minutes; the steam created in the covered bowl will help
loosen the skin from the flesh of the peppers. Uncover the bowl and
slip the skin off the peppers with your fingers. Even if you are
tempted to run the peppers under cool water to remove bits of
clinging skin, don't do it: You would be rinsing away the delicious
smoky flavor. If needed, use a clean towel to wipe away clinging bits
of skin from the peppers.

Cut the peppers in half, scoop out the seeds, stem, and any
membrane, and cut each pepper half in half again. Toss with ¼ teaspoon of the salt, ⅛ teaspoon of the pepper, and 1 tablespoon of
the olive oil.

Toss the zucchini with ¼ teaspoon of the salt and 1 tablespoon
of the olive oil. Grill the zucchini until it is browned lightly on the
outside and tender, about 2 minutes per side, turning once. Remove
to a platter.

recipe continues

Meanwhile, in a bowl, beat the ricotta with the pecorino, chives, and ¼ teaspoon of the salt. Adjust the salt if needed. The ricotta filling should be quite intense, since it will be layered with delicately flavored vegetables.

Lightly grease four 2-inch round ramekins. Line each with plastic wrap, letting the excess plastic wrap hang over the sides of the ramekins. Lay a slice of zucchini around the sides of each ramekin, covering the sides of the ramekins entirely but not overlapping, if possible.

Layer the roasted peppers with the ricotta mixture in the ramekins, making 5 layers in all; the bottom and top layer should be roasted peppers. Cover each ramekin with the overhanging plastic wrap and refrigerate for 30 minutes (or up to 12 hours). These are the millefoglie.

In a blender, blend the basil with the garlic, the remaining ¼ teaspoon of salt, and the remaining ¼ cup of olive oil until smooth. Unmold each millefoglie onto a plate. Spoon the basil sauce around the millefoglie and enjoy.

cooking with ricotta **Ricotta can be hit or miss: creamy and milky at its best, or chalky and thin at its worst. One way to get good ricotta is to buy it at an Italian market or cheese shop that gets it from a local cheesemaker; it will likely be thick in texture and rich in flavor, with very little whey to dilute the taste. The best ricotta is imported from Italy; much of it comes from Latium, and some is even made from sheep's milk (ricotta di pecora in Italian). If your local cheese shop carries it, by all means try it, or check the Mail-Order Sources (page 183). Avoid supermarket ricotta, which is sold in plastic tubs, since it will be watery and weak. If all you can get your hands on is thin, watery supermarket ricotta, transfer it to a cheesecloth-lined sieve set over a bowl and let it drain its excess whey overnight in the refrigerator. And, finally, opt for whole-milk ricotta if you have a choice. Ricotta is a very lean cheese, among the leanest produced anywhere in the world, even when it is made from whole milk.**

seared cabbage hearts with toasted caraway seeds

cuori di cavolo con semi di carvi tostati /// SERVES 4

1 medium Savoy cabbage
   (1 pound untrimmed weight)
3 tablespoons extra-virgin
   olive oil
¾ teaspoon salt
2 teaspoons caraway seeds
¼ teaspoon freshly ground
   black pepper

cook's note Savoy cabbage is a wrinkled, green variety with an earthier flavor and softer texture than regular white or red cabbage. Be sure to trim the dark, coarse outer leaves of the cabbage to uncover the delicate pale hearts. The trimmed weight of the cabbage should be around ½ pound.

I love this cabbage accompanied by rye bread slathered with fresh, unsalted butter and a glass of sparkling white wine. The caraway seeds are toasted to bring out their full aromatic potential, and the cabbage remains slightly crisp in the center after a few moments on a hot grill. It's a delightful side dish to grilled white fish or poultry, and it reminds me of flavors I encountered in Friuli–Venezia Giulia, a northeastern Italian region that touches upon Croatia, where cabbage and caraway seeds (locally called cumino dei prati, or "field cumin") are often paired to surprisingly delicious effect in soups and sautés.

Heat a grill to a medium-high flame.

Trim the bottom of the cabbage. Remove 6 to 8 outer layers to reveal the tender, pale cabbage heart. Cut the cabbage in half from top to bottom and then cut out the hard core (it looks like a pale, hard triangle) from each half, being careful to keep each half intact. Brush with 1 tablespoon of the olive oil and season with ¼ teaspoon of the salt.

Place the two cabbage halves, cut side down, on the grill. Cook for 5 minutes, or until the bottom is tinged with brown and the inside is starting to soften. Flip and cook the other side until it is also tinged with brown and the cabbage is almost soft all the way through, about 5 more minutes; some of the inner layers may still be crunchy. If so, cook a little longer. As the cabbage cooks, flatten it with a heavy spatula so more of it is exposed to the flames. If the cabbage starts to burn, move it to a cooler part of the grill.

Remove the cabbage from the grill and place on a cutting board. Cut into 2-inch pieces and place in a bowl.

In a small skillet set over medium heat, toast the caraway seeds, shaking the skillet often, until aromatic and a shade darker, about

2 minutes. Immediately remove the caraway seeds to the bowl with the cabbage (they may burn if left in the hot skillet). Add the remaining 2 tablespoons of olive oil, the remaining $\frac{1}{2}$ teaspoon of salt, and the pepper. Toss well to coat and adjust the seasoning if needed. Serve hot, warm, or at room temperature.

storing olive oil **As for most foods, heat and light are olive oil's natural enemies, causing the oil to deteriorate faster than it would otherwise and to oxidize, eventually becoming rancid. To slow down the inevitable deterioration process, store olive oil away from light and heat; a pantry far from the stove is ideal. You can store olive oil in the refrigerator if you don't plan on using it all up within a year of purchase (something I've actually never done, since I go through a few bottles a month!). The oil will turn cloudy and firm up in the refrigerator, but it will return to its normal, clear liquid state when it is brought back to room temperature.**

The average shelf life of olive oil is eighteen months from the date of bottling, as long as it is properly stored. Experts say you can tell if olive oil is rancid when it tastes like pumpkin (I find rancidity fairly easy to detect: The oil tastes bitter and aggressive on the palate and is no longer fruity in flavor, and the smell resembles that of motor oil). Some bottles of olive oil have a production date stamped on the label, but most do not, so you are better off buying your olive oil at a store that has a good turnover if you want to be sure the oil you buy was recently bottled. As olive oil ages, it loses its pronounced fruitiness and becomes more delicate in flavor. In the first few months after pressing, olive oil is pungent, fruity, and deep, and its color is dark, tending to green. Within four or five months, its flavor becomes a touch milder, its color less intense. After a year, the fruitiness gives way to a mellow olive flavor and the color changes to a golden hue. After eighteen months, much of the olives' aroma has dissipated and the color is far brighter, almost yellow.

sauces, marinades
and spice rubs

mayonnaise [PHOTOGRAPH ON PAGE 146]

maionese /// MAKES 2 CUPS

3 large egg yolks, at room
   temperature
1/2 teaspoon salt
1/4 teaspoon freshly ground white
   pepper
2 teaspoons fresh lemon juice
1 cup peanut oil, virgin olive oil,
   or extra-virgin olive oil

cook's note The eggs in a classic mayonnaise are raw, so be sure you buy fresh, preferably organic, eggs. If you are concerned about bacteria in raw eggs, prepare a cooked egg version of mayonnaise: Using a wire whisk, beat the egg yolks with 1/3 cup of cold water (no lemon juice yet) in a stainless-steel bowl over a pot of simmering water until the mixture becomes slightly stiff and frothy, about 30 seconds; remove from the heat and add the oil in a thin stream, then whisk in the lemon juice, salt, and pepper.

Homemade mayonnaise has little to do with the commercial stuff. Creamy, richly flavored, it is made with egg yolks only, as opposed to whole eggs, and quite a bit less oil than store-bought. Mayonnaise is the most common of emulsified sauces, essentially an emulsion of oil and water-based liquids (either vinegar or, more commonly in Italy, lemon juice). Since water and oil don't readily form a stable mixture, a third ingredient—usually egg yolks—is added to ensure they bind to each other (that's what an emulsion is). The water-based liquid (usually the acidic ingredient in mayonnaise) is added to the egg yolks, along with salt and pepper, and then oil is added drop by drop until the two bind; only when the emulsion has formed can the oil be added more quickly, or the mayonnaise may break (in other words, the oil and water base will separate). All the ingredients for mayonnaise should be at room temperature, or you may have difficulty forming an emulsion.

The oil you choose will have the greatest impact on mayonnaise's flavor. A flavorless oil like peanut oil will yield a pale yellow, mild mayonnaise; a fruity one like extra-virgin olive oil will produce a greenish, strongly flavored mayonnaise; and a virgin olive oil will result in a mayonnaise whose flavor falls somewhere between these two extremes.

Place the egg yolks in a large stainless-steel bowl with sloping sides. (Don't use an aluminum bowl for mayonnaise, or it will turn gray.)

Add the salt, pepper, and 1 teaspoon of the lemon juice. Beat the ingredients together using a wire whisk.

Place the oil in a measuring cup with a handle and a spout. Very slowly, teaspoon by teaspoon, add the olive oil to the egg-yolk base, whisking all the while. Wait for the oil to be combined with the egg-yolk base before adding any more, or the emulsion may not form; don't rush this process. When the yolk base and oil have started to thicken and the oil is no longer pooling in droplets at the surface, the emulsion has formed; at this point, start adding the oil in a thin, steady stream while you beat with the whisk. Continue to whisk in the oil in this manner until the mayonnaise becomes thick; you may not need all the oil. Add the remaining teaspoon of lemon juice, taste for salt, and adjust if needed. Refrigerate the mayonnaise until you are ready to serve it, but don't store it any longer than 48 hours.

flavored mayonnaise **Use home-made mayonnaise as the starting point for a host of flavorful sauces simply by adding well-chosen ingredients to the basic recipe. Below are some of my favorites.**

garlic mayonnaise **Crush 1 peeled clove of garlic with 1/4 teaspoon of salt in a mortar with a pestle; add to the egg-yolk base.**

herb mayonnaise **Add 2 tablespoons of minced fresh herbs—I favor tarragon or chives—to the egg-yolk base.**

saffron mayonnaise **Soak a pinch of saffron pistils in 1 tablespoon of hot water for 30 minutes; add both the water and saffron pistils to the egg-yolk base.**

spicy mayonnaise **Add 1/2 teaspoon of cayenne pepper to the egg-yolk base.**

mustard mayonnaise **Add 1 table-spoon of Dijon mustard to the egg-yolk base; since mustard is also an emulsifying agent, the mayonnaise will bind more easily.**

caper mayonnaise **Fold 1/4 cup of chopped capers and 2 tablespoons of minced Italian parsley into the finished mayonnaise.**

RAW TOMATO
SAUCE

PARSLEY-CAPER
SAUCE

MAYONNAISE

raw tomato sauce

salsa di pomodori cruda /// MAKES 2 CUPS

2 large, ripe beefsteak tomatoes
 (1¼ pounds), cut into ⅛-inch
 dice
1 medium purple onion, cut into
 ⅛-inch dice
¼ cup extra-virgin olive oil
⅛ to ¼ teaspoon cayenne
 pepper
2 tablespoons minced thyme
1 teaspoon salt

cook's note Season the tomatoes with salt just before serving, or they will exude a lot of water and dilute the flavor of the sauce.

My mother served this light, summery sauce often when I was growing up. It is wonderful with a thick, juicy steak, grilled pork chops, or firm-fleshed grilled fish like swordfish or tuna. The amount of cayenne pepper you add is altogether personal; add a lot for a searingly hot sauce or just a pinch for the merest hint of spice.

Toss the tomatoes, onion, olive oil, cayenne, and thyme together in a medium bowl. Add the salt just before serving and toss again. Serve at room temperature.

taming raw onions As much as I love onions, I sometimes find raw onions overpowering. Whenever I suspect onions to be too strong or acrid to be used raw in a salad or sauce, I use a cool-water soak to mellow them out.

To soak raw onions, cut the onions as needed, then soak in cool water to cover for 30 minutes or so: the water will draw out some of the onions' acrid flavor. Drain the onions thoroughly and blot dry, and proceed with your recipe.

parsley-caper sauce [PHOTOGRAPH ON PAGE 146]

salsa verde /// MAKES 2 CUPS

1 large hard-boiled egg (see
    sidebar)

1 cup packed cubed crustless
    white country bread

¼ cup white-wine vinegar, plus
    extra if needed

1¼ teaspoons salt

⅛ teaspoon freshly ground black
    pepper

3 cups packed Italian parsley
    leaves

¼ cup capers in brine, drained

3 salted anchovies, boned,
    gutted, and rinsed, or
    6 anchovy fillets packed in oil,
    drained

6 gherkins, chopped

2 garlic cloves, peeled

¾ cup extra-virgin olive oil

cook's note Be sure to use only parsley leaves in salsa verde. The stems
are quite bitter and must be carefully
removed.

Salsa verde, a classic green sauce made across Italy with minor and major variations, is used alongside boiled and roasted or grilled meats, poached fish, and other dishes that require a vibrant partner. Its base is always a generous dose of parsley (hence its name), a bit of garlic, some anchovies, olive oil, and vinegar—but the similarities end there. Some versions call for boiled and mashed potatoes as a thickener, instead of crustless bread; others incorporate olives instead of gherkins; and still others include pine nuts. This is the Piedmontese salsa verde, also known as bagnet verde, meaning "green bath."

Separate the hard-boiled egg white and egg yolk; place the yolk in a food processor (reserve the white for salads and garnishes).

Soak the bread with the vinegar for 5 minutes, then squeeze dry and crumble into the food processor. Add the salt, pepper, parsley, capers, anchovies, gherkins, and garlic. Activate the processor and process to a paste. With the motor running, add the olive oil in a thin, slow stream; the sauce should emulsify (become thick and creamy). Taste the sauce. If it is not tart enough, add a touch more vinegar in a thin, steady stream.

Transfer to a bowl and refrigerate for a minimum of 30 minutes (or up to 24 hours) before serving.

perfect hard-boiled eggs As elementary as it may seem, there is a technique to attain perfect hard-boiled eggs. A perfect egg has a creamy yet firm yolk, with no trace of gray or green around its rim. As with most things in the kitchen, it's all a matter of timing. Place the eggs in a pot, cover with 2 inches of tepid water, and bring to a boil over medium heat. As soon as the water boils, turn off the heat and cover the pot. Let the eggs sit in the hot water for 13 minutes exactly (the timing is important: any longer, and the yolk will develop that ugly gray-green ring; any less, and it may not be fully cooked). Immediately drain, cool, and shell.

light tomato sauce

sugo di pomodoro leggero /// MAKES 2 CUPS

2 tablespoons extra-virgin
olive oil

2 small shallots, halved and
thinly sliced

12 basil leaves

8 ripe plum tomatoes, peeled,
seeded, and diced (see
sidebar)

½ cup water

¼ teaspoon sea salt

⅛ teaspoon freshly ground
black pepper

cook's note If you like a chunky texture to your tomato sauce, don't purée
it in a blender.

There are hundreds of variations on tomato sauce across Italy. Some call for carrots and celery to be cooked along with the onion; others omit garlic; others still use butter or lard instead of olive oil. This is an all-purpose tomato sauce that pairs splendidly with grilled meats, fish, and seafood. It can be made in large quantities, especially in the summer, when fresh tomatoes are succulent, and frozen in sealed jars for later use.

Heat the olive oil in a 1-quart saucepan over a medium flame. Add the shallots and basil and cook until the shallots soften, about 10 minutes. Add the tomatoes, water, salt, and pepper, and cover; cook 30 minutes, stirring often, reducing the heat if needed to prevent scorching.

Transfer the sauce to a blender and purée until smooth, or use a food mill fitted with a medium disk if you prefer. Adjust the salt if needed. Serve, or cool to room temperature before freezing.

peeling and seeding tomatoes
To peel and seed tomatoes, bring 1 quart of water to a boil over medium heat. Make a small crosswise slit— about ½ inch—on the bottom of each tomato and cut away the stem at the top of each tomato. Drop the tomatoes into the boiling water. Cook until the skin starts to lift away from the flesh, about 2 minutes if the tomatoes are firm and a bit less if they are soft. With a slotted spoon, remove to a bowl of ice water; slip off the skins and drain. Cut the tomatoes in half widthwise (around the equator) and scoop out the seeds with your fingers. The tomatoes are now ready to be diced, minced, or cut into strips.

creamy grilled pepper sauce

salsa ai peperoni arrostiti /// MAKES 1–1½ CUPS

6 red bell peppers
2 garlic cloves, peeled
½ cup tightly packed mint leaves
12 drops Tabasco sauce
  (optional)
1¼ teaspoons salt
¼ teaspoon freshly ground black-
  pepper
½ cup extra-virgin olive oil

cook's note The sauce will keep in the refrigerator for up to 1 week, but it will thicken and take on a gelatin-like texture upon standing. If needed, swirl in a bit of olive oil before serving.

I love this sauce with grilled shrimp or chicken, as a dip for fennel or celery, or spooned atop crostini. You can use orange or yellow peppers instead of red for a different look. Or, for a truly elegant presentation, make both a red pepper sauce and a yellow one, spoon a bit of each on a plate, and use a toothpick to create a pretty swirl pattern where the two meet; a grilled chicken breast or grilled jumbo shrimp would look splendid atop this two-toned edible canvas.

Heat a grill to a high flame.

Place the whole peppers on the grill. Grill until the skin is blackened all over and the flesh is soft, 15 to 30 minutes, turning every few minutes with tongs to cook evenly. The peppers should be nearly collapsing when done.

Remove to a bowl and cover tightly with aluminum foil. Set aside for 30 minutes; the steam created in the covered bowl will help loosen the skin from the flesh of the peppers. Uncover the bowl and slip the skin off the peppers with your fingers. Even if you are tempted to run the peppers under cool water to remove bits of clinging skin, don't do it: You would be rinsing away the delicious smoky flavor. If needed, use a clean towel to wipe away clinging bits of skin from the peppers.

Cut the peppers in half, scoop out the seeds, stem, and any membrane, and chop coarsely. Place in a blender with the garlic, mint, Tabasco, if using, salt, and pepper. Process until smooth. Slowly add the olive oil in a thin, steady stream, and process until the sauce emulsifies. (You can make the sauce in a food processor too, but the blender will yield a creamier consistency.) Adjust the seasoning if needed and serve at room temperature. If the sauce thickens too much as it sits, stir in 1 tablespoon or so of olive oil before serving.

summer in a jar: storing grilled peppers

Strips of succulent grilled peppers tossed with nothing more than olive oil, slivered garlic, sea salt, and a few torn leaves of fragrant basil: summer on a plate. Accompanied by a hunk of crusty bread, a piece of pungent pecorino, a handful of olives, and a chilled bottle of white, you have a satisfying alfresco meal—or a taste of summer long after the season has passed.

When summer gardens and farmers' markets are bursting with sweet peppers, it's the perfect time to roll up your sleeves and make the most of the season's bounty. To store the grilled peppers in the refrigerator, pack them into glass jars, cover with extra-virgin olive oil, tuck 1 or 2 peeled garlic cloves and a handful of washed basil leaves in each jar, and refrigerate for up to 1 week. To freeze the peppers, place the peppers in plastic freezer-safe bags and freeze immediately (roasted peppers will keep in the freezer for up to 4 months).

herbed olive oil sauce for fish and seafood

salmoriglio /// MAKES 2 CUPS

1 cup extra-virgin olive oil

½ cup hot water

½ cup fresh lemon juice

½ teaspoon salt

¼ teaspoon freshly ground
black pepper

1 garlic clove, peeled and
smashed (see sidebar)

¼ cup minced Italian parsley

1 tablespoon minced oregano

cook's note Should you choose to marinate raw fish or seafood in salmoriglio (or any other acidic marinade) before grilling, limit the marinating time to 30 minutes: lemon juice breaks down fish, making it unpleasantly soft after extended marinating.

A savory olive-oil-based sauce for fish or meat, salmoriglio owes its very name to the salt that is one of its essential components. Salmoriglio is prepared across Italy, but it is most closely associated with southern regions, especially Calabria and Sicily, where it is usually brushed over fish, seafood, meat, poultry, and sausages as they cook over a live fire. A long oregano branch or sprig of rosemary may be used to dip into the salmoriglio and brush it over the food on the grill—efficient, environmentally friendly, and a great way of imparting flavor on the food as it cooks. At its most basic, salmoriglio calls only for olive oil, salt, and pepper; common embellishments include garlic, lemon juice or vinegar, and fresh herbs, especially oregano or mint. The version I offer here is Sicilian and can be used as a marinade for raw fish and seafood before it goes on the grill (just be sure to cool it first) or can be passed around the table, warm, to be spooned atop grilled fish and seafood.

Place the olive oil in a 1-quart heatproof bowl. In another bowl, combine the water and lemon juice; slowly pour the lemon juice mixture into the olive oil in a thin steady stream, beating all the while with a whisk or fork. Season with the salt and pepper, add the garlic, parsley, and oregano, and place the bowl over a pot filled with simmering water. It is important that the bottom of the bowl not touch the simmering water.

Heat the sauce gently for 3 to 4 minutes, or until just warm. Whisk again and serve warm as a sauce for grilled fish or seafood, or cool to room temperature and use as a marinade for fish and seafood before grilling.

smashed versus crushed garlic
Smashed garlic is simply peeled and then smashed once with a heavy knife to break it down slightly and allow some of its essential oils to seep out when it is cooked or added to a marinade or sauce; it still retains its integrity, and looks pretty much like a clove of garlic, only a bit flattened. Crushed garlic, on the other hand, is worked into a paste, usually with salt, either on a cutting board with the aid of a chef's knife or in a mortar with a pestle; it is creamy in texture and pungent in flavor. Adding salt helps break down the garlic into a paste quickly and easily. For a bare hint of garlic, use smashed garlic and pluck out the garlic later; for a bold garlic taste, use crushed garlic.

classic marinade for meat and poultry

marinata semplice per carne e pollame ///

MAKES ABOUT ½ CUP, ENOUGH FOR 2 POUNDS OF MEAT OR CHICKEN

¼ cup dry white wine

¼ cup extra-virgin olive oil

½ teaspoon Worcestershire sauce

¼ teaspoon cayenne pepper (optional)

½ teaspoon freshly ground black pepper

4 garlic cloves, minced

1 tablespoon minced thyme

1 tablespoon minced sage

1 tablespoon minced rosemary

1 tablespoon minced oregano

2 fresh bay leaves (optional)

Grated zest of 1 to 2 lemons

cook's note If you want to serve the marinade as a sauce with the grilled meat or poultry, transfer it to a small pot and bring it to a boil over a medium flame. Cook for 5 minutes to burn off the raw alcohol and, most importantly, to kill any bacteria transmitted to it by the raw meat.

My mother's marinade for roasted chicken combines white wine, olive oil, garlic, a hint of cayenne, and Worcestershire sauce. Over the years, I added lemon zest and fresh rather than dried herbs. Spatchcocked chicken (see pages 87–88) is the ideal meat to soak in this flavorful marinade, but veal chops, pork chops, and kebabs do beautifully too. Be sure to use a good wine in your marinade, as you will be able to taste it even after it's cooked.

In a bowl, whisk all the ingredients together; or place all the ingredients in a jar, seal with a lid, and shake vigorously. Place the meat or seafood in a large, shallow container and pour the marinade over it. Turn to coat well and refrigerate for 2 to 48 hours. Blot dry before grilling. Since the marinade does not contain any salt, season the marinated food with salt before grilling.

grating lemons and other citrus fruit A box grater is all you need to grate citrus zest. First, wash the citrus thoroughly, especially if it isn't organic. Dry it, and rub it up and down the box grater on the side with the finest holes. Stop as soon as you start to see white appear on the citrus—the white is the pith, and it is very bitter. You only want the vibrantly flavored zest that covers the pith. Some people cover the grater with a sheet of plastic wrap to prevent zest from getting stuck between the grater's holes, but I never bother—I just reach in and dislodge any zest that got caught in the holes after I'm finished grating.

mom and dad's chili sauce

salsa piccante di mamma e papa' /// MAKES 3 CUPS

12 long, medium-hot red chili peppers, chopped coarsely

10 garlic cloves, chopped coarsely

10 ripe plum tomatoes, peeled, seeded, and diced (see page 149)

2¼ teaspoons salt

2 tablespoons white-wine vinegar

3 tablespoons fennel seeds, coarsely crushed in a mortar

½ cup extra-virgin olive oil, plus extra to cover the sauce in the refrigerator

cook's note Dutch peppers most resemble the Italian peppers my parents use. Mildly hot, they are long, red, and a bit crooked. If they aren't available, try De Agua, Fiesta, or Fresno peppers instead. Each of these varieties has a different level of heat, so you may need to adjust the amount of chilies accordingly. In general, the smaller the pepper, the spicier it will be.

My dad is wild for this homemade sauce and eats it nearly every day. My mom came up with the recipe after a bit of trial and error. Dad knew what he wanted the sauce to taste like but didn't quite know how to go about it; he has only recently started to cook. My mom, an excellent cook with a particular talent for sauces, found just the right balance of spicy, sweet, and acid for him: Adding tomatoes sweetens the chilies' bite, while a bit of vinegar makes the sauce vivacious and bright. The fennel seeds are my dad's contribution. As the seeds sit in the sauce, they soften—so even if they seem a bit crunchy on the first day, they will mellow over time. If you are not too fond of fennel seeds, decrease the amount used, as this recipe calls for a lot.

Place the chili peppers, garlic, tomatoes, salt, vinegar, and 2 tablespoons of the fennel seeds in a blender (a food processor is fine as well, but will yield a coarser consistency). Process until smooth.

Transfer to a 1-quart pot, bring to a boil, and cook over medium-low heat for 30 minutes, stirring once in a while; the sauce should thicken somewhat. Cool to room temperature and stir in the remaining tablespoon of fennel seeds and the olive oil. Adjust the seasoning if needed: The sauce should be quite spicy and a bit salty, but not overwhelmingly so.

Transfer to clean jars, seal, and refrigerate for up to 1 week; I always pour a bit of raw olive oil over the sauce in the jar so it is protected from contact with the air. You can also freeze the sauce for up to 1 month. Serve with anything and everything grilled, as well as salads, bread, even pasta.

spice rub for fish and seafood

aromi misti per grigliate di pesce ///

MAKES 2½ TABLESPOONS, ENOUGH FOR 1¼ POUNDS OF FISH OR SEAFOOD

1 teaspoon salt
1 tablespoon dried oregano
1 tablespoon dried tarragon
1 teaspoon sweet paprika
1 teaspoon black peppercorns

cook's note Although I much prefer fresh herbs to dried, this recipe calls for dried herbs so that you may make the spice rub in large batches and store it in the pantry for future use. You can certainly use fresh herbs instead of dried (double the quantities in that case) if you use the rub immediately.

Whether or not I toss fish and seafood with a liquid marinade (olive oil, lemon or lime juice, and so on) or a dry spice rub before grilling depends on two factors: whether I have a few minutes to spare before the food needs to go on the grill, and whether I want a pure sea flavor or a spicy, herbal kick in the finished dish. Liquid marinades such as Salmoriglio (page 152) are a great vehicle for flavor if I can let the fish or seafood soak them up for at least 15 minutes. Otherwise, I opt for dry rubs like the one below.

Combine all the ingredients in a mortar and crush until powdery with a pestle (or grind in a clean spice grinder if you prefer). Store in a sealed jar for up to 2 months, away from heat and light. When you are ready to grill, rub the spices over fish or seafood; I find 1 tablespoon to be sufficient for ½ pound of fish or seafood. This recipe can be scaled up for a larger yield.

storing dried herbs and spices
Like all food, dried herbs and spices have a shelf life—longer than that of fresh herbs, admittedly, but not infinite. Purchase dried herbs at a store with a good turnover, or they may have been sitting on the shelf for months or even years (check the Mail-Order Sources, page 183). Store dried herbs and spices away from heat and light in sealed containers; they should keep this way for 6 months. The longer you store dried herbs and spices, the less aromatic they will become.

spice rub for meat and poultry [PHOTOGRAPH ON PAGE 15]

aromi misti per carne e pollame ///

MAKES 4½ TABLESPOONS, ENOUGH FOR 2½ POUNDS OF MEAT OR POULTRY

1 teaspoon salt

1 teaspoon black peppercorns

½ teaspoon dried red pepper
   flakes

1 tablespoon dried rosemary

1 tablespoon dried thyme

1 tablespoon dried sage

1 teaspoon dried marjoram

1 teaspoon wild fennel (see Note)

cook's note Wild fennel has a pungent flavor that mates perfectly with full-flavored meats and poultry. If you can't find it in a specialty market near you, check the Mail-Order Sources (page 183), or substitute an equal amount of crushed fennel seeds.

This is a classic Italian dry rub for meat and poultry. The flavors are reminiscent of the countryside in autumn, when the wild herbs are starting to dry on the bushes and all around is the scent of rosemary, thyme, and wild fennel.

Combine all the ingredients in a mortar and crush until powdery with a pestle (or grind in a clean spice grinder if you prefer). Store in a sealed jar for up to 2 months, away from heat and light, although the flavor will be most intense when freshly ground. When you are ready to grill, rub the spices over meat or poultry; 1 tablespoon should be enough for ½ pound of meat or poultry. Keep in mind that stronger flavored meats like lamb and beef can be spiced more heavily than delicate meats like veal, pork, and chicken. This recipe can be scaled up for a larger yield.

drying your own herbs **If you find yourself with an excess of fresh herbs at season's end, here's how to dry them for future use. Wash them, dry them thoroughly (I usually spread them out in a single layer on clean kitchen towels), then transfer to a tray. Set the tray out in a cool, dry room (preferably in the dark to better preserve the herbs' color) and leave them undisturbed until dried out—it should take 1 to 2 weeks, depending on the humidity in the room and the type of herb you are drying. Once dried, the herbs should be stored in clean sealed jars, away from heat and light; if you like, you can crush them with your fingers before storing them, but they will be more aromatic if crushed just before use.**

sweet
endings

apple wedges in warm cinnamon-scented caramel butter *trance di mela con burro caramellato alla cannella* 170

tuscan rosemary and raisin buns *pan di ramerino toscano cotto sulla brace* 172

amaretto-stuffed peaches with vin santo glaze *pesche farcite all'amaretto al vin santo* 175

orange-scented focaccia stuffed with hazelnut-chocolate cream *focaccia all'arancia con crema di nocciole e cioccolata* 176

rum-glazed panettone with whipped mascarpone *panettone glassato al rum con mascarpone* 160

pears glazed with barolo wine *pere al barolo* 162

honeyed bruschetta with gorgonzola *bruschetta al gorgonzola e miele* 164

caramelized blood oranges over creamy ricotta mousse *mousse leggera di ricotta con arance sanguigne caramellate* 165

summer fruit packets with moscato d'asti *frutta estiva al moscato d'asti* 168

rum-glazed panettone with whipped mascarpone

panettone glassato al rum con mascarpone /// SERVES 4

FOR THE WHIPPED MASCARPONE

½ pound mascarpone (preferably imported Italian)

¼ cup orange-blossom honey

Grated zest of 1 orange

2 tablespoons Grand Marnier

FOR THE BERRIES

1 cup raspberries

1 cup blueberries

12 medium strawberries, hulled and quartered

2 tablespoons sugar

3 tablespoons fresh orange juice

FOR THE PANETTONE

4 tablespoons (½ stick) unsalted butter

¼ cup rum

¼ cup sugar

Four 3-inch-thick wedges of panettone

This recipe was born after a holiday season had passed and I found myself with more panettone (see sidebar) than I had bargained for. I couldn't imagine throwing the panettone out, so I devised a new way to enjoy it. If the urge to make this dessert strikes after panettone season has passed, you can grill slices of any sturdy cake, such as pound cake, instead.

Make the whipped mascarpone: In a large bowl, beat all the ingredients together with a whisk until smooth. (This can be done up to 12 hours ahead; refrigerate until needed.)

Make the berries: Toss the berries with the sugar and orange juice in a medium bowl up to 15 minutes before serving (if they are combined too long ahead of serving, the berries will become soft).

Make the panettone: Combine the butter, rum, and sugar in a small pan. Place over medium-high heat and cook until the butter has melted, about 2 minutes; the mixture will foam and bubble. Remove from the heat.

Brush the butter glaze over the panettone, coating both sides well. There will be some leftover glaze.

panettone, milan's venerable sweet **Panettone is Milan's quintessential Christmas cake. Baked since the Middle Ages, it was likely born in a Milanese bakery when a young baker tried to impress his boss's daughter by adding eggs, butter, and candied fruit to a simple yeasted dough. Legend has it that the young baker's name was Toni, hence the name panettone (from pan de Toni, or Toni's bread). More than six hundred years after its appearance, panettone is still offered as an edible gift to friends and acquaintances across Italy every holiday season. Buttery, eggy, moist, and light, panettone is delicious on its own or dunked into creamy cappuccino, and it stays fresh for months thanks to a natural yeast sponge. Similar to panettone, but less rich and without candied fruit, is the star-shaped pandoro of Verona, also a Christmas specialty.**

Heat a grill to a medium-high flame.

Grill the panettone until golden brown on both sides and slightly caramelized, about 2 minutes per side, turning once and basting once or twice with the leftover butter glaze; remove to a serving platter. Do not cook over too high a flame, or the panettone may burn and taste unpleasantly bitter if the sugar and liquor in the glaze burn.

Serve the grilled panettone hot, topped with a dollop of the whipped mascarpone and a spoonful of the berries with their macerating liquid.

cook's note Instead of the bright opulence of berries, you can scatter wine-poached dried fruit over the panettone and mascarpone for a more subdued presentation. Combine 1 cup of dry red wine, 1 cup of water, 1/4 cup of sugar, a strip of lemon zest, and 1 cinnamon stick in a 2-quart pot. Bring to a boil over medium heat, stirring, then add 2 cups of dried apricots and 2 cups of dried pitted plums. Cook uncovered for 20 minutes, or until the fruit is soft and the poaching liquid has reduced to a thick, shiny glaze.

pears glazed with barolo wine

pere al barolo /// SERVES 4

1 cup Barolo

1 cup water

¼ cup sugar

1 cinnamon stick

1 strip of orange zest

2 ripe pears, peeled, halved, and cored

2 slices of brioche, challah, or other sweet, eggy bread, cut into 1-inch cubes

2 tablespoons (¼ stick) unsalted butter

cook's note When you reduce the Barolo poaching liquid from the pears, watch carefully that it doesn't scorch or burn. Sugar is highly susceptible to burning, so don't walk away during this critical step.

The inspiration for this sweet comes from Piedmont, where my parents now live and where I spent weekends and summers since I was a child. Not only does Piedmont offer beautiful pears, its wines are among Italy's most prized, with Barolo ranking among the world's greatest wines. A rich, robust red made from Nebbiolo grapes in the hills around the town of Barolo, it is best aged five to eight years and aerated two hours before serving. This recipe is the perfect vehicle for a bottle of young Barolo: No need to open a vintage wine that costs a fortune.

If using wooden skewers, soak 8 wooden skewers in water to cover for 30 minutes; drain.

In a 1-quart pot over medium heat, bring to a light boil the Barolo, water, sugar, cinnamon stick, and orange zest, stirring often.

Add the pear halves and cook until not quite tender when pierced with a knife, 8 to 10 minutes (the riper the pears, the faster they will cook). Don't overcook the pears at this stage, or they will fall apart on the grill later.

Remove the pears from the poaching liquid with a slotted spoon and cool to room temperature (reserve the liquid). Cut into 1-inch cubes and thread onto the skewers, alternating a cube of pear with a cube of bread; this is a delicate operation, so be gentle to avoid breaking the pears or bread and causing them to fall off the skewer. There may be leftover bread.

Return the poaching liquid to a gentle boil over medium heat and reduce it until it becomes thick and shiny, like a glaze, 5 to 10 minutes. Don't burn the poaching liquid; lower the heat to prevent scorching if needed. Swirl in the butter and remove from the heat. Discard the cinnamon stick and orange zest. This is the Barolo glaze.

Heat a grill to a medium flame.

Brush the pear and bread skewers with some of the Barolo glaze. (Reserve the rest of the glaze.) Place the skewers on the grill and cook until the bread is crisp on the outside and the pears are lightly browned around the edges, about 5 minutes, turning as needed to cook evenly and removing them from the grill before they burn. (Sugar burns easily, so pay close attention.)

Pool the remaining glaze on each of 4 plates. Serve the pear skewers hot, on top of the glaze.

preventing wooden skewers from burning **When grilling food on wooden skewers, there is always a risk that the skewers will burn, even if you have soaked them in water to cover for 30 minutes prior to using. Soaking does lessen the chance of burning, but won't eliminate it entirely, especially if the flame is high or the skewers cook for a relatively long time. To prevent skewers from burning, line the grate with a piece of aluminum foil, placing it where the bottom (the exposed part) of the skewers will be; the grate should be free of aluminum foil (that is, fully exposed) where the skewered food will come into contact with it. Lay the skewers on the grate, resting the exposed wood on the aluminum foil.**

honeyed bruschetta with gorgonzola

bruschetta al gorgonzola e miele /// SERVES 4

Four 1-inch-thick slices of
   country bread
1/2 pound gorgonzola dolce,
   crusts removed, at room
   temperature
4 teaspoons white truffle honey
   (see Note) or other honey

cook's note Truffle honey is a surprising ingredient. I discovered it a few years ago, when I held a truffle cooking class and wanted to introduce the taste of truffles in a dessert course. I drizzled it over chunks of aged pecorino toscano to great effect. The best truffle honey is infused with shavings from the white truffle, *Tuber magnatum pico;* check the label to be sure you are buying the real thing (the words *Tuber magnatum pico* should be written clearly), and be prepared to spend a good sum of money—then take a whiff and let yourself be transported to the dewy hills of Piedmont in autumn. As with all truffle products, a little goes a long way. To buy white truffle honey, check the Mail-Order Sources (page 183).

Over the past few years, restaurants in Italy have started offering cheeses paired with varietal honeys, preserves, and wines as an alternative to the standard dessert course. I love the idea of mating savory cheeses with sweet honey and preserves, and I have come up with a few pairings I adore, like this one, which can be savored on its own or atop slices of grilled country bread. I love white truffle honey with gorgonzola and other pungent cheeses, but you can substitute wildflower, clover, or any other honey you like.

If the slices of bread are very large, cut in half or quarters as needed; I like to present slices of about 2 to 3 inches in length.

Heat a grill to a medium-high flame.

Spread the gorgonzola evenly on the bread; you may not need all of the gorgonzola depending on the size of your bread.

Grill the bread, gorgonzola side up, for 2 minutes, or until the bottom is browned and the gorgonzola is just starting to melt. Transfer to a platter and drizzle immediately with the honey. Serve hot.

sweet bruschetta inspiration Assuming you are as much of a fan of bruschetta as I am, here are some more sweet bruschette to try.

mascarpone-jam bruschetta Whip mascarpone and your favorite jam until smooth, then spread atop bread. Grill until lightly crisp on the bottom.

chocolate bruschetta Finely chop bittersweet chocolate; fold it into whole-milk ricotta and spoon atop bread. Grill until lightly crisp on the bottom.

berry bruschetta Using a fork, crush berries with sugar and grated orange zest until soft; spoon atop bread. Grill until lightly crisp on the bottom.

caramelized blood oranges over creamy ricotta mousse

mousse leggera di ricotta con arance sanguigne caramellate /// SERVES 4

[PHOTOGRAPHS ON PAGES 166–167]

FOR THE RICOTTA MOUSSE
¾ pound whole-milk ricotta
¼ cup chestnut honey
Grated zest of 1 lemon
12 mint leaves, minced

FOR THE CARAMELIZED
ORANGES
2 blood oranges
¼ cup sugar

TO SERVE
2 tablespoons Grand Marnier

cook's note The ricotta you use in this dessert should be thick and creamy, not watery. If you suspect your ricotta is watery, set it in a cheesecloth-lined sieve over a bowl in the refrigerator for a few hours, topped with a plate to press out the extra whey. The best ricotta can be found in cheese shops rather than supermarkets and should be used within a day or two, as it is highly perishable and will develop an unpleasant tang if stored too long.

This Sardinian-inspired recipe combines a classic trio, chestnut honey, lemon zest, and mint, often incorporated in cheese-based desserts on the island. Chestnut honey has a bitter edge and a very particular flavor. I love it, but the reaction of some people has led me to decide that it's an acquired taste. If you aren't fond of bitter honey, use a sweeter honey like orange-blossom or lavender. If at all possible, get your hands on Sicilian blood oranges rather than California blood oranges: Not only is their vermillion color more striking, but their flavor is so much more intense. And, should you ever decide to cut them into segments, the sturdier membranes of Sicilian blood oranges make the tricky job less perilous.

Heat a grill to a medium flame.

Make the ricotta mousse: In a large bowl, whisk all the ingredients together until smooth. Divide among 4 wide-mouthed glasses and refrigerate. (This can be done up to 12 hours ahead.)

Make the caramelized oranges: Using a sharp knife, peel the skin and bitter white pith away from the oranges; the oranges should still hold together as perfect, bald spheres. Cut into ¼-inch-thick round slices. Spread the sugar out on a plate. Dredge the orange slices in the sugar, coating both sides well.

Grill the orange slices until golden on both sides and lightly caramelized, about 2 minutes per side, turning once; remove to a platter. Be careful not to cook the orange slices on too hot a flame, or the sugar will burn rather than simply caramelize. (This can be done up to 1 hour ahead, but be sure to save the delicious juices the oranges exude after grilling.)

When you are ready to serve, spoon the caramelized orange slices over the ricotta mousse in the goblets. Splash with the Grand Marnier and serve immediately.

caramelized blood oranges over creamy ricotta mousse [RECIPE PAGE 165]

sugar-dipped grilled fruit **For a simple—and simply irresistible—dessert, heat a grill to a medium flame and cut up a variety of fresh fruit. Try ripe summer peaches, nectarines, and plums, halved and stoned; large strawberries, preferably with the stems on; thick wedges of mango; and halved figs. Scatter 1 cup of sugar on a tray and dredge the fruit in the sugar; place on the hot grill and cook until the sugar starts to caramelize and the fruit exudes some of its glorious juices, about 2 minutes for small or soft fruit (strawberries, figs) and 4 minutes for larger or firm fruit (peaches, plums, nectarines). Serve hot, arranged on a platter with bowls of cool marscarpone for dipping if you wish. Be careful to moderate the flame on the grill to prevent the sugar from burning rather than caramelizing on the fruit.**

summer fruit packets with moscato d'asti

frutta estiva al moscato d'asti /// SERVES 4

12 medium or 8 large
    strawberries, hulled

2 ripe peaches, 3 ripe plums, or
    3 ripe apricots, pitted and cut
    into large, strawberry-size
    chunks

3 ripe figs, quartered

4 tablespoons (½ stick) unsalted
    butter, cubed

¼ cup Moscato d'Asti

¼ cup sugar

⅛ teaspoon ground cinnamon
    (optional)

cook's note Moscato d'Asti is a wine everyone seems to love. Made from aromatic Muscat grapes, it is low in alcohol, lightly fizzy and sweet, and just perfect for spiking homey desserts or for sipping after a rich meal. To purchase it by mail, check the Mail-Order Sources (page 183).

I came up with this recipe years ago, when I returned from the market with an abundance of summer fruit and little time to make a dessert for guests who were coming to dinner. I had grilled vegetables in foil packets before, but never before attempted fruit; I wasn't sure how the heat would affect the delicate fruit and was concerned about it turning out mushy and watery. The result was wonderful, and the presentation a lot of fun—in fact, this is probably the recipe in the book that most surprised my husband and me. The important thing to remember when grilling fruit in packets is to keep the flame high: if the fruit cooks too slowly, it will be mushy and watery. As soon as the foil packets swell and balloon, it's time to remove them from the heat.

Any seasonal fruit can be cooked this way, but strawberries, figs, and stone fruit like peaches and plums have great affinity for the grill. In the winter, I often cut grapefruit in half and dot them with butter and brown sugar, then grill them, cut side down, in foil packets, just until they start to caramelize; it's an idea I borrowed from my friend Maria Pacheco Doria, one of the owners of Grace's Marketplace in Manhattan and a fabulous Italian cook.

Halve the strawberries lengthwise if they are large; leave them whole if they are medium. In a large bowl, toss all the ingredients together and set aside to macerate for 30 minutes. This draws out the sugars in the fruit.

When you are ready to serve, heat a grill to a high flame.

Cut sturdy aluminum foil into four 8-inch lengths. Place the foil, shiny side up, on a work surface. Top each piece of foil with one quarter of the fruit mixture, including the macerating liquid, and fold in half to enclose into tight bundles. Be sure the edges are sealed or the liquid will cause flare-ups on the grill if it leaks out.

Place the foil bundles on the grill, seam side up, and cook for 3 to 4 minutes, without turning; if you turn the bundles, the liquid might leak out and cause flare-ups on the grill. The fruit is ready when the bundles inflate dramatically. Serve hot, opening the bundles at the table for the most spectacular effect, and enjoy with spoons rather than forks to better savor the delicious cooking juices. Try spooning a dollop of vanilla ice cream over the fruit inside the packets for an indulgent summer treat.

more ideas for grill-roasted fruit **Fruit cooks up splendidly in an aluminum foil roasting pan atop a grill. Here are some ideas:**

bananas Peel and split bananas in half lengthwise. Place in an aluminum foil roasting pan atop a grill with unsalted butter, walnuts, and sugar, and grill-roast for 5 minutes, or until just softened. Serve with vanilla gelato.

pears Peel, halve, and core pears. Place in an aluminum foil roasting pan atop a grill with dry white wine, sugar, and a strip of lemon zest, and grill-roast for 10 minutes, or until soft. Serve topped with gorgonzola and a drizzle of honey.

apples Peel, quarter, and core apples. Place in an aluminum foil roasting pan atop a grill with Marsala, pine nuts, currants, and a cinnamon stick; drizzle with honey and grill-roast for 10 minutes, or until soft.

figs Place whole fresh figs in an aluminum foil roasting pan atop a grill with a touch of Vin Santo (see page 175), a light dusting of sugar, and a handful of slivered dried apricots. Grill-roast for 5 minutes, or until soft.

plums Halve and pit ripe plums. Place in an aluminum foil roasting pan atop a grill with dry red wine, sugar, and a strip of orange zest; grill-roast for 10 minutes, or until soft.

apple wedges in warm cinnamon-scented caramel butter

trance di mela con burro caramellato alla cannella /// SERVES 4

4 firm, sweet apples, such as
  Gala or Golden Delicious

$1/2$ cup heavy cream

$1/2$ cup plus 2 tablespoons sugar

2 tablespoons water

2 tablespoons ($1/4$ stick) unsalted
  butter

$1/16$ teaspoon ground cinnamon

cook's note It's important to cook the apples a few minutes in boiling water before grilling them, or the outside will be burned by the time the inside is cooked. If you like, you can flavor the poaching liquid with a star anise, a cup of sweet wine such as Moscato d'Asti, and a strip of orange zest before dropping in the apples.

One of the clearest memories I have of my grandmother Eva is of her peeling fruit. She had a special way of peeling every fruit: oranges in lengthwise segments, figs in delicate curls. I still peel apples the way she did, just as my father does: Cut each apple in clean quarters, core each quarter, and then carefully cut away the peel. No need for fancy corers and peelers—just a table knife and a bit of patience. These grilled apples are a perfect fall dessert: easy to prepare, and infused with the comforting taste of autumn. Leftovers (in the unlikely event you have any) are delicious chopped up and spooned inside a sweet pastry shell for an apple pie.

Cut the apples into quarters, and cut out the core and seeds from each quarter, and peel each quarter.

Bring 2 quarts of water to a boil in a 3-quart pot. Add the apple wedges to the boiling water and cook for 4 minutes, or until crisp-tender. Drain and rinse under cool water to stop the cooking. (To flavor the water before boiling the apple wedges, see Note.)

In a small skillet, heat the cream to the boiling point over a medium-high flame. Keep warm.

In a clean, heavy-bottomed 1-quart pan, combine $1/2$ cup of the sugar and the water. Set over medium heat and cook until the sugar caramelizes, about 5 minutes, stirring once in a while. Stir in the butter (be careful to avoid splattering), then the hot cream and cinnamon. Whisk all the ingredients together for a few seconds and remove from the heat.

Heat a grill to a medium-high flame.

Roll the boiled apple wedges in the remaining 2 tablespoons of sugar, coating well on all sides.

Grill the sugar-coated apple wedges until the sugar caramelizes and the apples are golden all over, about 4 minutes, turning as needed to cook evenly. Be careful not to burn the apples; the sugar coating may scorch if the heat is too high or the apples are not turned quickly enough. Remove to a platter.

Gently warm the caramel butter for a few seconds over low heat. Pour the warm caramel butter over the grilled apple wedges and serve hot.

tuscan rosemary and raisin buns

pan di ramerino toscano cotto sulla brace /// MAKES 8 BUNS

⅓ cup raisins, soaked in warm
   water to cover for 30 minutes
2 large rosemary sprigs
¼ cup extra-virgin olive oil, plus
   extra for greasing the bowl
2 cups unbleached all-purpose
   flour, plus extra for the work
   surface
1 teaspoon instant yeast
¼ cup sugar
½ teaspoon salt
About ⅔ cup warm water (110°F.)

cook's note Old Tuscan recipes
don't call for plumping the raisins in
water before cooking them in the oil,
but I find the soak makes them softer.
You can also try plumping the raisins in
sweet wine or Vin Santo (see page 175)
instead of water.

Tuscans have been baking raisin-studded loaves for Lent for centuries. Initially, the recipe yielded large loaves and wasn't enriched with oil or sweetened with sugar. Nowadays, the raisins are cooked in olive oil in which a whole rosemary sprig has been warmed, and the dough is split into small portions to yield hand-size buns. The buns—and the original large loaves baked for Lent—are traditionally slashed with a cross shape, which the devout took as a religious symbol but which, in fact, merely helps the bread not to split during baking. By grilling rather than baking the buns as is Tuscan custom, the rosemary flavor is intensified—a happy thing for someone who loves rosemary as much as I do!

Drain the raisins and blot them dry on clean paper towels.

In a small pan, place 1 whole rosemary sprig, the raisins, and the olive oil. Cook over low heat until the rosemary aroma infuses into the oil, stirring once in a while, about 5 minutes. Discard the whole rosemary sprig. Cool to room temperature.

Finely mince the leaves of the remaining rosemary sprig; you should have about 1 tablespoon (mince more rosemary if needed).

Mix the flour, yeast, sugar, and salt in a food processor (if your food processor comes with a plastic blade, use it instead of the metal blade). With the motor running, add enough of the warm water to obtain a dough that holds together and forms a ball around the blade. Process for 45 seconds, adding a little more water if the dough is dry or a little flour if it is sticky. The dough should be smooth, supple, and silky.

Lightly oil a bowl, place the dough in it, shape into a ball, turn to coat with the oil, and cover with plastic wrap. Let rise at room temperature until doubled, about 1 hour. (Or refrigerate and let rise up to 24 hours; return to room temperature before proceeding.)

When the dough has doubled, turn it out onto a work surface (there is no need for flour on the work surface, as the dough will be so oily that it won't stick). Knead the raisins along with their cooking oil and the minced rosemary into the dough. It might be difficult at first, as this is quite a bit of oil and the dough will feel slippery, but the dough will eventually absorb the oil and raisins.

Cut the dough into 8 pieces. Shape into eight ½-inch-thick disks on a lightly floured work surface, trying to push the raisins beneath the surface of the dough or they may burn on the grill. Cover the buns and let rest for 30 minutes.

Heat the grill to a medium flame.

Transfer the buns directly to the grill. Cook for 8 minutes, or until the bottom is very lightly browned and the dough looks like it is starting to cook in the middle. Flip using a set of tongs. Cook for 8 minutes more, or until the bottom crust is lightly crisp and just golden and the inside is cooked all the way through. If the buns brown too quickly before they have a chance to cook through, move them farther away from the flame and cook more slowly over indirect heat. Cool on racks to prevent the buns from becoming soggy; serve warm or at room temperature.

tips for successful grilled breads **The main challenge when grilling bread is to ensure that the inside of the bread cooks through before the outside burns. Therefore, keep the flame relatively low, and if needed, move the bread to a cooler part of the grate if you suspect it is cooking too fast. Remember that larger breads will take longer to cook through than smaller ones, and will therefore require lower heat to avoid burning the outside. To test bread for doneness, thump it on the bottom: If it sounds hollow, it is done. You can also insert a thermometer into the thickest part of the bread; bread is fully cooked when it registers 200°F.**

amaretto-stuffed peaches with vin santo glaze

pesche farcite all'amaretto al vin santo /// SERVES 4

4 ripe but firm peaches, halved
  and pitted, peel on

¼ cup sugar

½ cup crumbled amaretti (about
  4 large amaretti)

2 tablespoons (¼ stick) unsalted
  butter, at room temperature,
  plus extra for greasing the
  roasting pan

1 large egg

½ cup water

½ cup Vin Santo

cook's note Amaretti are almond macaroons, crunchy and dry and laced with bitter almonds. Piedmont is the region of Italy best known for its amaretti. When I was little, my parents bought large quantities wrapped in multicolored paper, which they offered to guests in a dramatic glass bowl. Aside from being a favored dessert, amaretti are used in numerous savory recipes in northern Italy and often appear in fillings for fresh pasta or stuffed roasted vegetables such as baby onions. Look for them in specialty markets or purchase them through the Mail-Order Sources (page 183).

The Piedmontese and Ligurians are known for their amaretto-stuffed roasted peaches. They are truly sublime as long as the fruit is ripe and sweet. (If you have any doubts about the peaches you are using, substitute another ripe fruit instead.) Cooking the stuffed peaches directly on the grill would dry them out and yield burned-on-the-outside, raw-on-the-inside fruit; placing them in an aluminum foil roasting pan with a bit of Vin Santo, a Tuscan dessert wine, allows them to cook to perfection. If you don't have Vin Santo on hand, substitute Marsala, a fortified dessert wine from Sicily.

Heat a grill to a high flame.

Scoop out some of the peach flesh around where the pit used to be, dice finely, and place in a bowl. Add the sugar, amaretti, butter, and egg, and crush with a fork.

Arrange the scooped-out peach halves, cut side up, in a 12-inch aluminum foil roasting pan. Stuff each with some of the amaretti mixture. Pour the water and the Vin Santo into the pan around (but not over) the peaches. The liquid should come no more than a third of the way up the peaches.

Place the roasting pan on the grill and cook until the peaches are tender but still hold their shape, 25 to 30 minutes. If the peaches are very ripe, they will cook through faster; test them to be sure you don't overcook them, or they will become mushy. The Vin Santo and water should have reduced to a light glaze; if the mixture evaporates or starts to burn, add a bit more water to prevent scorching.

When the peaches are done, remove them with a slotted spoon to a platter. If needed, reduce the glaze in a small pot over medium-high heat until it is thick enough to coat the back of a spoon. Serve at room temperature, drizzled very lightly with the glaze.

orange-scented focaccia stuffed with hazelnut-chocolate cream [PHOTOGRAPH ON PAGE 179]

focaccia all'arancia con crema di nocciole e cioccolata

[PHOTOGRAPH ON PAGE 179]

MAKES 8 FOCACCIAS

- ½ cup whole milk, plus extra if needed
- 2 cups unbleached all-purpose flour, plus extra for the work surface
- 1 teaspoon instant yeast
- ¼ cup sugar
- ¼ teaspoon salt
- 4 tablespoons (½ stick) unsalted butter, at room temperature, plus extra for greasing the bowl
- Grated zest of 1 orange
- 1 large egg
- 24 Gianduiotti chocolates (see Mail-Order Sources, page 183)

cook's note Be careful not to over-heat the milk for the dough. If the milk is hotter than 120°F., you risk killing the yeast, resulting in heavy, doughy focaccia dough that won't rise. Yeast is temperature-sensitive and should be activated by liquids at about 110°F. For additional tips on working with yeast, see page 45.

In this recipe, a rich, buttery bread dough is rolled out into disks and cooked over a gentle fire, yielding plump focaccias that are then split and slathered with a melted hazelnut chocolate known as Gianduiotti. (For a less expensive—yet far less elegant—alternative to the Gianduiotti, you can simply use room-temperature Nutella, a hazelnut chocolate spread.) If the marriage of orange and chocolate is heavenly, it becomes pure perfection by adding hazelnuts. In order for the focaccia not to burn, yet to have the time to cook all the way through, it is essential to cook it low and slow: This is the sort of dough that would have been cooked over the dying embers of a spent fire. Regulate the heat carefully and, if the focaccia seems to be taking on too much color, move it to a cooler part of the grill.

Make the focaccia dough: Warm the milk to 110°F. Mix the flour, yeast, sugar, and salt in a food processor (if your food processor comes with a plastic blade, use it instead of the metal blade). With the motor running, add the warm milk, then the butter, orange zest, and egg. Process for 45 seconds, adding a little milk if the dough is dry or a little flour if it is sticky. The dough should be smooth, supple, silky, and a bit tacky to the touch.

Lightly butter a bowl, place the dough in it, shape into a ball, and cover with plastic wrap. Let rise at room temperature until doubled, about 1 hour. (Or refrigerate and let rise up to 24 hours; return to room temperature before proceeding.)

Heat the grill to a medium-low flame.

Meanwhile, unwrap the Gianduiotti chocolates and place in a stainless-steel bowl over a pot of simmering water. Heat gently until melted and smooth, stirring often with a rubber spatula. Do not overheat or the chocolate will curdle.

Cut the dough into 8 pieces. Shape into 8 balls on a lightly floured work surface. Cover and let rest for 15 minutes (this allows the gluten to relax, making stretching easier). Using a rolling pin (or your hands for a lighter texture), roll into $3^1/_2$-inch circles; the circles should be about $^1/_4$ inch thick.

Transfer the circles directly to the grill. Cook for 10 to 15 minutes, or until the bottoms are very lightly browned and the dough looks like it is starting to cook in the middle. Flip using a set of tongs. Cook for 10 to 15 minutes more, or until the bottom crusts are lightly crisp and golden, and the dough is cooked all the way through. If the focaccias brown too quickly before they have a chance to cook through, move them farther away from the flame, to a cooler spot where they can cook more slowly over indirect heat. Remove to a platter and, using a sharp serrated knife, cut the focaccias in half horizontally.

Slather the melted chocolate over the bottom half of each focaccia, top with its own lid, and serve hot, warm, or at room temperature.

bitter and sweet, a chocolate tale Chocolate's Latin name, *Theobroma cacao*, means "food of the gods," a fitting description for a food so well loved. Derived from the tropical cocoa tree, chocolate was first consumed as a bitter, energizing drink by native Indian runners; it held such an esteemed role in Maya culture and religious rites that the Maya were even buried with jars of cocoa. When it was introduced in Europe in the sixteenth century, chocolate became a fashionable drink in high-society salons, where it was often flavored with chili or vanilla, as it had long been by the Maya. In 1644, a Roman physician named Paolo Zacchia wrote about chocolate, tracing its origins from the Indies to Portugal and on to Italy. By the late seventeenth century in Florence, hot and cold chocolate drinks were sold in small earthenware beakers, and the ruler Cosimo de' Medici's physician had written of experiments with flavorings for chocolate; these included ambergris, citron, lemon, musk, and jasmine. Italian cooks soon started exploring the culinary possibilities of chocolate in dishes both sweet and savory. There were polentas topped with grated chocolate, chocolate ice creams, chocolate-studded nougat, and chocolate sauces for game (such as the grand Sicilian chocolate sauce for seafood caponata, known as Salsa San Bernardo). Chocolate became a favored vehicle for poison, and it is believed that Pope Clement XIV was poisoned with chocolate in 1774—a bitter end for a man who had suppressed the chocolate-loving Jesuits only a year earlier.

orange-scented focaccia stuffed with hazelnut-chocolate cream [RECIPE PAGES 176–177]

suggested menus

When I wrote this book, I wanted you to be able to create entire meals—antipasto through dessert—on your grill. After all, once you've got the flame going, you may as well use it to its fullest potential. We rarely think of the grill in terms of appetizers, first courses, and desserts—but whether it's a humble bruschetta rubbed with a cut tomato, or polenta topped with a creamy gorgonzola sauce after a brief interlude on the grill, or fruit tossed with sugar and sweet wine in a tightly sealed aluminum foil packet, there's an infinity of dishes both savory and sweet that you can enjoy hot off the grill.

To create a full-blown grill menu, pick something from a few different chapters: an appetizer or first course, followed perhaps by a vegetable and a fish or meat dish, then a dessert to close the meal. When mixing and matching recipes, strive for contrast in color and texture, and avoid repeating ingredients in the same menu. Balance the dishes in terms of richness, and try to serve the food in a crescendo of intensity: start off with milder dishes and work your way up to more vibrant, stronger flavors. Here are some menus for various occasions.

sicilian summer

bruschetta with chopped tomatoes, tuna, and capers (page 22)

sicilian pepper bundles (page 120)

swordfish bundles with sicilian orange and pine nut stuffing (page 77)

fresh fruit

tuscan feast

tomato-rubbed bruschetta (page 21)

herb-crusted tuna steak with arugula and cherry tomato salad (page 60)

fresh fruit

vegetarian alfresco

fire-kissed tuscan bread and tomato salad (page 135)

eggplant coins with chunky walnut—chive salsa (page 124)

focaccia stuffed with mascarpone and truffled olive oil (page 52)

summer fruit packets with moscato d'asti (page 168)

savoring sardinia

sardinian eggplant purée with white wine and garlic (page 122)

lobster, lemon, and mint salad (page 79)

sardinian smoked lamb (page 104)

bread

caramelized blood oranges over creamy ricotta mousse (page 165)

lazy brunch

savory sausage and sweet grape skewers (page 95)

young goat cheese and smoked prosciutto coins (page 27)

espresso

taste of central italy

smoky flatbread (page 48)

selection of cheeses

chicken stuffed with fennel and prosciutto (page 84)

tuscan rosemary and raisin buns (page 172)

elegant entertaining

summer vegetable millefoglie in basil oil (page 137)

sea scallops with tri-color pepper medley and slivered basil (page 71)

baby lamb chops in garlic, green peppercorn, and mustard marinade (page 103)

seared asparagus with lemon zest and chives (page 127)

pears glazed with barolo wine (page 162)

mail-order sources

Please see the next page for corresponding mail-order sources for these special ingredients.

condiments, dried goods, and luxury items

Amaretti **1, 2, 4, 7, 10, 14, 24**

Balsamic and wine vinegars **1, 2, 4, 7, 8, 10, 12, 14, 24**

Bread flour **16**

Canned Italian plum tomatoes **1, 2, 4, 7, 8, 10, 12, 14, 24**

Cornmeal **1, 2, 4, 7, 8, 14, 16, 24**

Gianduiotti **1, 2, 4, 7, 14, 24**

Instant yeast **16**

Italian wines **13, 19, 22, 28, 29**

Oil-preserved porcini mushrooms **1, 2, 4, 7, 8, 14, 24**

Olive oil **1, 2, 4, 7, 8, 10, 14, 24**

Pane carasau **2, 4, 7**

Polenta **1, 2, 4, 7, 8, 14, 16, 24**

Salted anchovies **1, 2, 4, 7, 14, 24**

Salted capers **1, 2, 4, 7, 14, 24**

Spices and herbs **20**

Truffles and truffle products **1, 2, 4, 7, 8, 9, 10, 14, 24, 25**

Varietal honeys (white truffle and others) **1, 2, 4, 7, 9, 10, 14, 24, 25**

perishables (meat, fish, and produce)

Game (wild boar, rabbit, hare, etc.) **7, 9, 14, 27**

Fish and seafood **7, 14, 17, 27**

Full range of produce **10, 14, 18**

Italian sausages **2, 7, 10, 14**

Porcini mushrooms (fresh, frozen, dried) **4, 9, 10, 14, 25**

cured meats, cheeses, and dairy products

Buffalo's-milk mozzarella **1, 2, 4, 7, 10, 11, 12, 14, 24**

Caciocavallo **1, 2, 4, 7, 10, 11, 12, 13, 14, 24**

Cured meats (including pancetta, speck, prosciutto cotto, prosciutto di Parma, prosciutto di San Daniele) **1, 2, 4, 7, 10, 12, 14, 24**

Full range of cheeses **1, 2, 4, 7, 10, 11, 12, 14, 24**

Italian butter **2, 4, 7, 10, 14**

Scamorza **1, 2, 4, 7, 10, 11, 12, 14, 24**

equipment

Grilling equipment **3, 5, 6, 15, 21, 26, 30**

Smoking and grilling woods **3, 5, 6, 15, 21, 26, 30**

Specialty kitchen items **5, 6, 15, 16, 23, 26**

1. A.G. Ferrari Foods
3490 Catalina Street
San Leandro, CA 94577
(510) 346-2100
www.agferrari.com

2. Agata & Valentina
1505 First Avenue
New York, NY 10021
(212) 452-0690

3. Blue Moon Woods
P.O. Box 207
2350 Sopchoppy Highway
Sopchoppy, FL 32358
(888) 959-9291
www.bluemoonwoods.com

4. BuonItalia
75 Ninth Avenue
New York, NY 10011
(212) 633-9090

5. Char-Broil
P.O. Box 1240
Columbus, GA 31902
(800) 241-7548
www.charbroil.com

6. Charcoal Companion
7955 Edgewater Drive
Oakland, CA 94621
(800) 521-0505

7. Citarella
2135 Broadway
New York, NY 10023
(212) 784-0383
www.citarella.com

8. Colavita USA
2537 Brunswick Avenue
Linden, NJ 07036
(908) 862-5454
www.colavita.com

9. D'Artagnan
280 Wilson Avenue
Newark, NJ 07105
(800) 327-8246
www.dartagnan.com

10. Dean & DeLuca
121 Prince Street
New York, NY 10012
(212) 254-8776
www.deandeluca.com

11. DiBruno Brothers House of Cheese
930 South Ninth Street
Philadelphia, PA 19147
(215) 922-2876
www.dibruno.com

12. Formaggio Kitchen
244 Huron Avenue
Cambridge, MA 02138
(888) 212-3224
www.formaggiokitchen.com

13. Gotham Wines & Liquors
2517 Broadway
New York, NY 10025
(212) 932-0990
www.gothamwines.com

14. Grace's Marketplace
1237 Third Avenue
New York, NY 10021
(212) 737-0600
www.gracesmarketplace.com

15. Grill Lover's Catalog
P.O. Box 1300
Columbus, GA 31902
(800) 241-8981
www.grilllovers.com

16. King Arthur Flour Company
P.O. Box 876
Norwich, VT 05055
(800) 827-6836
www.bakerscatalogue.com

17. Legal Sea Foods
One Seafood Way
Boston, MA 02210
1-800-EAT-FISH
www.sendlegal.com

18. Melissa's
P.O. Box 21127
Los Angeles, CA 90021
(800) 588-0151
www.melissas.com

19. Panebianco Imports
1140 Broadway, Fifth floor
New York, NY 10001
(212) 685-7560

20. Penzeys Spices
P.O. Box 933
Muskego, WI 53150
(800) 741-7787
www.penzeys.com

21. Peoples' Woods
75 Mill Street
Cumberland, RI 02864
(800) 729-5800
www.peopleswoods.com

22. Sherry-Lehmann
679 Madison Avenue
New York, NY 10021
(212) 838-7500
www.sherry-lehmann.com

23. Sur La Table
1765 Sixth Avenue South
Seattle, WA 98134
(800) 243-0852
www.surlatable.com

24. Todaro Brothers
555 Second Avenue
New York, NY 10016
(212) 532-0633

25. Urbani USA
2924 Fortieth Avenue
Long Island City, NY 11101
(718) 392-5050
www.urbani.com

26. Weber-Stephen Products Company
200 East Daniels Road
Palatine, IL 60067
800-446-1071
www.weberbbq.com

27. Wild Edibles
318 Grand Central Terminal
New York, NY 10017
(212) 687-4255

28. Winebow
22 Hollywood Avenue, Suite C
Ho-Ho-Kus, NJ 07423
(800) winebow
www.winebow.com

29. WineWave
100 Jericho Quadrangle
Suite 343
Jericho, NY 11753
(516) 433-1121
www.winewave.com

30. W W Wood, Inc.
P.O. Box 398
Pleasanton, TX 78064
(830) 569-2501

acknowledgments

Creating a cookbook requires far more than just an author, and it always amazes me how kind and generous people are with their time and knowledge when their expertise is called upon in such a project.

I am so thankful to the creative team at Clarkson Potter for the splendid job they have done with this book. A heartfelt thank-you to Pam Krauss, whose wisdom is equaled by her kindness and professionalism; Chris Pavone, my editor, whose boundless energy, intuition, and passion for his work makes collaborating such a pleasure; Adina Steiman, for helping on more levels than I can enumerate; Marysarah Quinn, creative director, and Jane Treuhaft, designer, for transforming my manuscript into a work of art; Mark McCauslin, production editor, Felix Gregorio, production manager, and Tammy Blake, publicity director, for all their hard work.

I am indebted to Ron Manville for his beautiful photographs, and to Roscoe Betsill, food and prop stylist, for his incredible eye. My agent, Judith Riven, deserves an enormous thank-you: Since we met years ago, she has been so much more than an agent to me.

At Grace's Marketplace in New York City, I owe a debt of gratitude to everyone in the Doria and Pacheco families. Thank you to Grace Doria and the late Joe Doria senior for their belief in me, and to Maria Pacheco Doria, whose kitchen has become my second home. Thank you to Rusty Pacheco for his expertise, and to Paul Fusco for his helpful advice. A big thank-you to all my students at Grace's for making teaching such a joy.

At the Institute of Culinary Education in New York City, a heartfelt thank-you to Rick Smilow and the staff. I thank everyone at Central Market, Doralece Dullaghan at Sur La Table, Arlene Ward at Adventures in Cooking, LaVerl Daily at Le Panier, and Jim Dodge, general manager at the Getty Museum in Los Angeles.

I thank Jack Cacciato at WineWave, LynnMarie Salata, Davide Pinzolo, and Michael Green. At Colavita, I am indebted to John Profaci and Jennifer Lionti; and at Citterio, Joe Petruce and Tony Bartolemeo.

I am so appreciative of Arlyn Blake and Anna Nurse at the James Beard Foundation; Cesare Casella of Beppe Restaurant in New York City; and David Leite of Leite's Culinaria. In Texas, thank you to Lori, Efisio, and Francesco Farris; at World Publications, Steve Blount; at *Bon Appétit,* Barbara Fairchild, Kristine Kidd, and Monica Parcell; and at *Cooking Light,* Krista Montgomery and Ann Pittman. Everyone at the Italian Trade Commission in New York, Montreal, and Toronto deserves to be thanked for their hard work.

For his unwavering support and love, I thank Jerry Ruotolo. I also thank Susanna Saarinen, Sal Rizzo, Julie Brasil, Ouathek Ouerfelli, Robert Ruotolo, Bianca Bianco, Abby and Rudi Weid, Ric Cohen and Karen Chandross, Ari and Keren Sandman, and Jen and Uli Iserloh for their friendship.

As I wrote this book, I was inspired by the many barbecues I enjoyed with my family when I was little. I thank my parents, Mony and Gabriella, for giving me life, a love of food, and an appreciation for beauty.

My deepest appreciation goes to my husband, Dino De Angelis. He is my best friend, my most astute judge, and my biggest supporter. If not for his love and understanding, I would be a different person—and this book may never have come to be.

index

Page numbers in *italics* refer to photographs.